The Love Motive

The LOVE MOTIVE

A PRACTICAL PSYCHOLOGY
OF SANCTIFICATION

Jon Tal Murphree

CHRISTIAN PUBLICATIONS

Camp Hill, Pennsylvania

To my mother
in whose saintly soul and practical life
I have consistently observed
the living Christ.

Christian Publications
3825 Hartzdale Drive, Camp Hill, PA 17011

The mark of ✝ *vibrant faith*

ISBN: 0-87509-422-8
LOC Catalog Card Number: 89-82275
© 1990 by Christian Publications
All rights reserved
Printed in the United States of America

94 93 92 91 90   5 4 3 2 1

CONTENTS

FOREWORD

A FEW YEARS AGO DURING A CONFERENCE I was assigned to a nice European hotel. That it was an unusual lodging became apparent the first evening when I noticed shoes placed outside the door of virtually every guest room except mine. I had seen this practice on a limited scale before, and knew that for a charge the porter would collect the shoes during the night, returning them freshly shined in the morning.

After a day or so I commented to a friend that I had never been in a place like this where the people got their shoes polished every day. He looked at me curiously and asked, "What's so strange about that?"

"It's too expensive," I replied. "I can't afford it."

He looked at me in astonishment. "Don't you know that in this hotel shoe care is included in the price of the room? You are paying for the service whether you use it or not."

You may be sure that thereafter I put my shoes out like everyone else. Yet because of my ignorance, for a while I walked around with scuffed shoes looking like a tramp when I was entitled to a first-class shine.

Many times I have thought that is the way it is so often with the beauty of holiness. Our Lord has purchased this right for every child of God, but through misunderstanding, if not unbelief, many Christians live as second-class citizens in the kingdom.

Much of the problem comes through confusion regarding the basic meaning of sanctification, especially in understanding the natural qualities of our human nature as contrasted to the sinful, self-centered, carnal disposition. Because the distinctions

1

are fuzzy, many Christians have no confidence or victory in their witness.

That is why I am grateful for this book. It comes to grips with practical issues in the quest for heart purity, and without depreciating persons with different theological presuppositions, helps clarify the meaning of personal holiness.

Giving the account a ring of authenticity is the author's own ministry as pastor, evangelist and college professor. He loves people. He also loves Jesus, and the single-hearted desire to please Him becomes the bottom line in what he writes.

Reading these lines will make Christian sainthood more reasonable. I hope, however, that no one will be content with mere understanding, but that knowledge will be confirmed in a living experience of the reality.

Robert E. Coleman

INTRODUCTION

THE NOTION OF CHRISTIAN SANCTITY is surrounded by much argument and confusion. Exaggerated claims by proponents have caused strong reaction, so much so that many Christians have despaired of its possibility. Consequently, pessimism regarding sanctification has become part of some theologies. Even among those who embrace its possibility, little has been done to implement it in a practical way in people's lives.

More recently, with the advent of secular theology, there has been a societal shift toward secularizing the sacred. Even religionists have held personal piety up for ridicule.

In this volume I am building on two important assumptions. First, without overlooking human depravity as secular humanists have generally done, the idea of Christian sanctity is superbly *optimistic* about human potential. Second, rather than being monastically mystical, sanctification can be intensely *practical*, an integral part of successful living in our kind of world.

This volume is not intentionally controversial. It is not an apologetic polemic. The world has already been saddled with enough divisive disputation on the subject. Here the intent is to be conciliatory, with hopes that opposing views may find common ground. My effort is to clarify the notion of Christian holiness in a practical way, to give searching Christians a resource for daily living.

These pages reflect my personal quest for practical piety. In order to accommodate my own need, I have defined sanctification in motivational terms.

While these definitions do no violence to scriptural notions, I insist they are usable for the average Christian.

Some who read will disagree with my premises and presuppositions. Those persons have my high regard. While holding their own views, however, they should receive from this volume something both positive and practical to help them in their pilgrimage with Christ. This is my prayer.

For valuable suggestions and special encouragement, I am indebted to my colleague at Toccoa Falls College, Professor Donald E. Ratcliff, an astute scholar and author in behavioral science.

And for writing the foreword, I feel special appreciation to my former seminary professor Dr. Robert E. Coleman, distinguished author, educator and conference speaker around the world, whom I hold in high regard and deep affection.

Jon Tal Murphree

The Long Quest

B Y THE TIME I GOT TO MY OFFICE, my mind was churning up all the imagined ways I had been mistreated that morning. It was during my two-day fall break from college teaching. After our children had caught the school bus, I thought my wife and I could sit together leisurely for a few minutes before attacking the day ahead. Instead, she picked up the women's section of the morning newspaper and began reading.

I did what I thought any self-respecting man should do to let her know that I had things to do too—I went to the bathroom to shave. When I returned she was in the middle of her kitchen chores, her classical music station turned so high that it was hard to talk. I took the garbage out, gave her the usual good morning kiss and left.

Now I was sitting at my office desk reliving the episode, feeling self-pity at the way I thought she had treated me. The more I thought about it, the angrier I got. What she had done was a little thing, but I had blown it out of proportion. Ironically, as I thought about the incident I already had my Bible in hand for morning devotions. Before looking into God's Word, I was fanning the flames of anger.

When I finally came to my senses, I felt foolish.

This was so unlike my usual mental state. Years earlier my life had pivoted on a radical commitment—a deliberate decision to activate my desire to please Christ as my strongest controlling motive. Other desires had been reordered and preempted by this deep love motive. To a degree, I had developed attitudes and a lifestyle that centered on the desire to please Christ.

For the last 30 minutes, however, I had been operating from my surface desire to please self. When I realized what I was doing, perhaps with the Holy Spirit's prompting, I quickly switched over to my desire to please Christ. The circuit breaker was thrown on my surface desire, and I was free to shift back to my deep-level operating base. My unholy anger then had no ground to stand on and could make no claim for itself, and it soon melted away.

Before long something quite unexpected happened. The cobwebs in my mind were cleared away. I remembered how my wife, Sheila, had gotten up early to bake biscuits for the family, though she had been up late the night before. She had tiptoed quietly to the closet for her housecoat so that I could have 30 extra minutes of sleep. And I had been so preoccupied with myself that I had overlooked her loving sacrifice. I felt so stupid!

Is doctrine practical?

How and where do such practical situations plug into the biblical doctrine of Christian sanctification? Is the doctrine pure theory with no practical value? Am I expected to prevent such emotional reactions in order to achieve Christian sanctity? Or am I expected to have a religious experience that will preclude such reactions? Can a heart condition of holiness be retained when there are mild deflections of emotions, actions or attitudes?

Reared in a Christian home, I accepted Christ as my Savior at an early age. I was exposed as a youth to both the Calvinist tradition in the local Baptist churches and the Wesleyan tradition in Methodist churches. I heard that salvation was of grace through faith alone, quite apart from practical ethics. This made sense, but some extremists carried it too far, using it as a license for sub-Christian lifestyles. For me, this antinomianism left me with a conscience problem even if my eternal life were secure. Salvation could not be exclusively for the future. I wanted to be saved *from* my sins, not *in* my sins. I had a taste of heaven in my heart, and I was unwilling to settle only for a heaven in the future.

When I was confronted with the Wesleyan understanding of Christian sanctification, I quickly rejected it as a combination of hero mentality and pharisaic attitude. Some "sanctificationists" seemed mystical, almost monastic, while others emphasized their religious experience to the point that it had little practical application. Some seemed interested in a "second work of grace" as an end in itself, quite apart from living a good life.

Yet I could not oppose the broad notion of holiness if it referred primarily to being good. The bottom line was ethical. If Wesley's notion of Christian perfection was supposed to mean sinless perfection (as it was often misinterpreted to mean), I had no complaints about it on ideological grounds. Whether it was possible was another matter entirely. But surely no one could criticize the notion as a worthy ideal.

In college I decided the biblical language of "sanctification" and "holy living" generally referred to more than some kind of "positional relationship" that would allow a sinful heart condition to remain while covered by an atonement that places one in a "position" of holiness. This sounded like a game of pretense, as if God were using the atonement merely as a blindfolding apparatus. The entire force of Scripture came down on the side of ethics, character, genuine righteousness and real goodness. God's redemptive activity struck me as a courageous move to restore humankind to goodness and godliness rather than simply to herd people into heaven.

I heard the arguments over whether sanctification entailed the elimination of what was variously called carnal nature, inbred sin or inherited depravity. But I had trouble distinguishing between my depraved nature and my legitimate human desires through which temptation came so easily.

My quest continued. I came at sanctification from every angle I could imagine. I searched my own heart and life. I studied the Scriptures. I read theology. I listened to the testimonies of others. I heard claims for Christian holiness that could not possibly be authenticated. But I refused to reject a religious truth because of its worst advocates. Many times I thought I had reached the point of Christian sanctity, only to be disillusioned.

Discovery!

One night, in the beautiful campus grove of maples and walnuts at Asbury College, I struck serendipity! My love for Christ was activated as never before. Instantly I realized I was in virgin territory and that I could never have entered there alone. I had been led by a divine hand.

Pleasing Christ became a genuine desire and a driving motive. It was something to do rather than something to feel, something practical rather than something theoretical. It was a program for Christian holiness—a love program. It gave me a handle for sanctification, and I latched on to it.

My discovery involved what I consider to be an appropriate redefinition of some terms, but it does not violate any of the traditional categories or concepts. It is not a new theology. It simply makes distinctions that may prevent some of the excessive claims of an older terminology, without watering down the substance of sanctity.

The coming chapters reflect my understanding of what Christian sanctification should mean. And I believe the substance of what I say can be experienced and lived out in a meaningful way even by those Christians who may feel uncomfortable with sanctification terminology.

The New Motive

WHEN TONYA FELL IN LOVE WITH JASON, she soon discovered that she had a new motive to transcend much of her old life. It was liberating.

Mr. Doler faced old age feeling unloved and unappreciated. He became slothful, undisciplined and indulgent, with little reason to aspire toward good and noble enterprises. Then one of his small grandchildren took a special interest in him, and it dramatically altered his value system. Now he was a role model, his life was worth something and he had a reason to be good and to do right. As with Tonya he had acquired a new motive that was both inspiring and liberating.

Second-grade Donald performed poorly in school under a teacher who showed little interest in him. Halfway through the school year, a new teacher came to Donald's class. She gave him special attention, complimented his good work and expressed genuine happiness when he did well. Now he had a motive that resulted in excellent grades.

How personality ticks

The examples above show how human personality is motivated by relationships. In this book my purpose is to define sanctification in motivational or relational terms. This method does not, however, contradict the notion of the miraculous. Psychological explanation simply recognizes that God works through structures that He Himself has built into human personality. To be miraculous does not necessarily mean something is too gaseous for analysis. Explaining something psychologically is quite different from explaining it away. Of course, false psychology is just as false as false theology or false natural science. But correct psychology as well as correct theology or physics points us to God's truth. To explain sanctification in practical terms, we first need to take a cursory look at human personality and how it is best motivated.

The study of human personality began with Sigmund Freud. In Germany and America psychology had focused on human consciousness and behavior. Freud rejected this approach, focusing rather on subconsciousness and personality. He concluded that the development of human personality is basically physiological in nature.

Later students of human personality have variously defined it as a product of social relationships. Erich Fromm saw personality as a result of a person's drive for security in social structures and the tension between that drive and the desire for freedom. Erik Erikson depicts personality as the sum of all psychosocial confrontations with one's social environment. Carl Rogers's humanistic approach sees personality as conditioned by an individual's ideas of what others think of him or her. Henry Stack Sullivan pushed the relational model to new frontiers. He sees human personality as an unreal abstraction, nothing more than a hypothetical structure used to explain human behavior. To him, the irreducible unit of personality is primarily a field of relationships.

Traditional Judeo-Christian thought has held people to be more than fields of relationships. Instead individuals are thought of as centers of consciousness and self-consciousness. They have a measure of freedom and are conceptual beings with rational intellect. They are transcendent spirits, aspiring toward God. They are ethical creatures, both morally alive and morally accountable. People are substantive entities, created as individual units, "somebodies" rather than "nobodies," more than composites of parts or clusters of predicates. The person is a self or an ego or a personality center.

We must recognize, however, that the holistic personality unit does not exist apart from predicates or qualities that characterize the person. One such distinguishing mark that is essential to personality is what we call *sociality* or *sociability*. We are by nature social beings, characterized by the drive, the urge, the desire to relate with other people. This element is so essential to human personality that without it one can scarcely be human. The relationship may be romantic, fraternal, filial or paternal. It may be platonic, neighborly, esoteric or exoteric. But the urge to relate is essentially a part of humanness.

This differs from Sullivan's interpersonal approach, which defines personhood exclusively in terms of relationships. I have included in the definition of personhood the *desire to relate* and the emotional equipment for relating, not the relationships themselves. A human self is a personality entity quite apart from social relationships, but not apart from sociality. Being social means having the desire and capacity for social relationships. The *way* a person relates determines what the person is like. But only the propensity to relate is required for being a person. Personhood is defined—partially—in terms of being social in nature rather than having social relationships.

Why is there such a thing as loneliness that stings, torments and burns with iciness? The feeling of loneliness implies that people need fellowship and that without it they are incomplete and unfulfilled.

Why are physical pain and discomfort so much easier to bear when we know that someone cares? Why is grief mollified and grieving persons comforted by the sympathy and understanding of others?

Why do we long to share our successes and triumphs with others? A child is excited over a special recognition in school, and she cannot wait to get home to tell her mother. My daily activities seem always to be left hanging until I share them with my wife.

Created in God's image

Being social is one of the ways we were created in God's image. The social nature of God has often been overlooked, but it is expressed in the doctrine of the Trinity with a clarity that is difficult to miss. The Trinitarian relationship is so intimate, so mutually reciprocal, allowing for such a oneness between Father, Son and Spirit that the three exist not alongside each other but in and through one another. Yet they retain their individuality without which there could be no relationship. Polytheistic religions have had the notion of separate divine personalities, but only Christian Trinitarian monotheism can express the idea of perfect relationship.

Among Christians there is general consensus that God is by nature loving. If this is true then He has always been loving, even before the existence of any created beings. But love requires an object. There is no way God could be loving without someone to love. God could have had the capacity to love, but this is quite different from loving and having love. Of course, the problem is resolved in the Trinity. This expresses how God has always been a God of love.

We have often said that love is the primary moral attribute of God. If love is defined in the contemporary American way as little more than sentimental indulgence, certainly the word is inadequate for describing God's nature. But if it is defined in moral terms as it is in Scripture, then love must be near the heart of God's character description. At least most other divine attributes relate to love relationships.

Justice is another attribute of God. It is defined as one's attitude and actions—fairness, impartiality, equitability—toward other people, and therefore it has to do with relationships. God is also holy and good, both of which are matters of moral principle. But most moral principles have to do with relationships, either with God, other people or oneself.

Motivated by relationships

Furthermore, we have scriptural evidence that divine history is a history of love more than anything else. God is known for having acted out of love relationships. The motive for all He has done regarding humankind has been derived from love relationships. His purpose for creating the human race was for fellowship. He acted courageously and with great personal sacrifice in the process of human redemption in order to restore relationships. He answers prayer "for Jesus' sake" and at times for the sake of the relationship He has with the one who prays. It is startling to realize that at times *we ourselves* can move God to action.

Perhaps it reflects again our image of God that we are motivated by relationships. We are social creatures as He is a social Creator, and consequently we, like God, are motivated by relationships.

When Tonya fell in love with Jason, her new motive sprang from a new relationship. Mr. Doler's new motive from the grandchild's interest was from a new relationship. Donald's new motive for schoolwork came from a special relationship with the new teacher.

It is in the dynamo of relationships that motives are born. The most beastly acts of barbarity are products of hate relationships, and the most daring, selfless, sacrificial acts of courage spring from love relationships. Suicide is often the product of broken relationships, and vicarious sacrifices of voluntary death result from honored relationships.

The sanctification motive

If human motivation is primarily a matter of relationships, it is not surprising that we should look for the sanctification motive *in a special love relationship with God.*

Meaningful relationships with other people may sometimes liberate us from the self-centered motives that govern our lives, but they are inadequate to replace them. The human spirit has been equipped for a higher relationship than human ones, and without the liberating love relationship with God, the old immoral motive keeps erupting in other relationships.

Possibly there exist some selfless people who care nothing for Christ, people who live neither for Christ nor for self but for a spouse, for a son or daughter, for humanity in general or for a moral principle. They have discovered a motive strong enough to liberate them temporarily from the self-motive, but it is not the Christ-motive, so there is not Christian sanctification.

Whatever you desire most in life captures you and becomes your god. But no god lesser than God is big enough to be your god. In the end it will let you down. Lean too heavily and it will give way. Only God is big enough—beautiful, loving and appealing enough—to sustain your motive to live right. The desire to please Him grows on you. All the lesser loves that preempt your love for Christ are enslaving, but Christ-love is liberating from every other entanglement. Richard Lovelace wrote:

> If I have freedom in my love
>   And in my love am free,
> Angels alone, that soar above,
>   Enjoy such liberty.[1]

The whole notion of an unthreatened love relationship with God is not only justified in Scripture, but it is the highest scriptural ideal. More than that, though, it is the most imperative responsibility placed on humankind. "Love the Lord your God with all your heart" (Deuteronomy 6:5) speaks of having a heart that is undivided and a love that is unthreatened. It is stated specifically, both in the

Hebrew Shema and by Christ Himself, as the first and foremost commandment. If there is any one law that we must not rationalize away, this is it!

Pleasing Christ

W HEN OUR SON MARK WAS IN GRADE SCHOOL, his
Christmas list preparation matched that of any
other child. A BB gun was at the top of his list one
particular year, but that was not all. He had a long
list, and the closer we got to the big day, the more the
list absorbed his attention. Over and over again he
said, "Dad, I really want a BB gun for Christmas."

One evening after the announcement had been
repeated several times, he paused in reflection and
coughed up a candid confession: "Dad, I really don't
want to *want* so much!"

Being human we find it impossible not to want.
Even when we are wanting not to want, we are still
wanting. Sanctification is not a cessation of desire.
The idea is not to stop wanting, but to redirect one's
wants, to replace inferior desires with worthy ones.

During my teenage and college years, I struggled
with holiness, wanting to "be holy" for so many inadequate reasons. First, I thought I should do it for
conscience's sake — it was something I knew I ought
to do or be. On the face this is not an unworthy
motive; I might have made a case for this being the
most worthy reason for being good — goodness for its
own sake, simply because it is good.

But as a controlling motive for my life it did not

work. It was a worthy ideal, but for me it was non-functional. Trying to operate from this motive alone left me with a guilt trip. Then I discovered it was not the motive that did not work. Rather it was *me* that did not work—from this motive. I needed a reason for goodness and righteousness that was more motivational.

Appealing to self

Later, I found what I thought to be a more dynamic reason for Christian holiness in an appeal to my self-image. I wanted to be good, not for goodness's sake, but for my own. I wanted to be that kind of person. I wanted to feel good about myself. In a sense it was like being my own idol. This was probably less worthy than the original motive, but it was more powerful. It fired me deeply.

Yet again I discovered that I had latched onto a motive that failed the practical test. It let me down. The ideal was so far beyond the real that I could not attain such a self-image. Every prop I placed under it collapsed. Attempting the good life was frustrating, and it left me disappointed.

For Christ's sake

Then came the night in the college grove. What I discovered there was the *love* motive to please Christ *for Christ's sake*—not simply for goodness's sake or for my own sake. And it was not so much the motive to *do good* or to *be holy* or to *attain sanctity* for Christ's sake, but more to *please Christ* for His sake. Of course, pleasing Christ *is* doing good and being holy, but the goodness-holiness motive is absorbed in the desire to please Christ. The "pleasing Christ" desire includes the "being good" desire. It increases and intensifies the motive to be holy. Suddenly I was relating with a person instead of a principle. The desire was personal, warm and tender, not cold, calculated and mechanical.

I also realized that sanctification did not mean that I had to *relish* the inconvenience of being good. To the contrary, it meant a willingness to *accept* that inconvenience for the sake of pleasing Christ. I discovered I could be good and do right for Christ's sake. This gave me a handle for holiness. The change of focus marshalled my energies with a desire that was interpersonal and therefore motivational.

Pleasing Christ

Loving someone necessarily means that you want to please that person. I am hard put to find a more specific way to express love than to please and make happy the ones I love. Living from the "love for Christ" motive means specifically the desire and effort to please Him.

On first thought, the idea that I could actually please Christ seems ridiculously presumptuous. Who am I that I could bring either pleasure or pain to Him? To think He would stoop to allow His feelings to be affected by one like me requires insanity. Surely my experience was nothing more than a stupendous ego trip!

Yet in that moment under the walnut trees, I thought I sensed a divine smile, and that smile was purifying. Self-centered motives and unholy feelings melted under that smile. Hardly even aware of myself, I was conscious primarily of His feelings. And that consciousness was liberating me from preoccupation with my own feelings. My desires were so attached beyond myself that I was aware of neither pride nor humility. Whatever feeling I was experiencing, I seemed totally oblivious to it.

When I became aware of my feelings again, they seemed so unmixed, so untainted, so undivided. The desire was to please Him, and the sense of satisfaction from His smile was not that *I* had pleased Him, but that *He* was pleased. It was for His sake.

Later on when I focused back on those feelings analytically, the experience both supported my self-esteem and was at the same time humbling. And the self-esteem had come precisely from the humbling experience—not that I was important enough to please Him, but that I was servant enough, dependent enough, creature enough to please the Creator. But even here the focus was on His being pleased—not as a child is pleased by his father, but as a father is pleased by his child, a king by his servant or a master by his subject.

The feeling was akin to the feeling I had as a child after I had worked hard on a chore assigned to me by my father. My dad expressed great delight in my accomplishment. Whatever pride I had was not opposite humility. It was more like shamelessness. What bolstered my self-esteem was not primarily that I had done well, but that *my dad* thought I had done well. He had made the job assignment, and I was working for him. I did not glory in what I had done as much as I gloried in his approval. I was happy that he was happy with me. I was prizing his opinion more than my work. My pride was in his delight, not in my accomplishment. The accolade he gave me was humbling, leaving no place for vanity.

Still it seems audacious to suppose we can please Christ. Perhaps the word "acceptable," as used in Psalm 19:14 (KJV), "acceptable in Thy sight," would be more modest. Yet the Scriptures assure us that "we are God's workmanship" (Ephesians 2:10) and all things are "created . . . for Thy pleasure" (Revelation 4:11, KJV). The Psalmist was so bold as to announce, "He delighted in me" (Psalm 18:19).

God has stooped to make Himself vulnerable. Relating with us, He left His feelings unguarded allowing Himself to be affected by His creatures. I who have crucified Him am given the privilege of contributing to His pleasure. The One who died under my sins now delights in my love!

Perhaps the primary ingredient in Christian holiness — pleasing Christ — is also the greatest pleasure in heaven. To be recognized by God, to be "delighted in" by Christ, to contribute to His pleasure — what greater experience could we ask? Perhaps Christian sanctity provides for the Christian an advance deposit of heaven in the heart, a "foretaste of glory," an appetizer for the eternal banquet!

Finding the motive

Recently a college student said to me, "I have tried to love God enough to put Him first, but I just don't. I know I should, but I don't know how. How can I love God?"

Like most other responsibilities, it is easier said than done. The question is: Is it something we do or is it something He does in us? The answer is both.

The big problem is with our corrupted self-love that we call carnal nature. We love ourselves in such sickly, unhealthy ways that we have no heart to love Him. The two loves are incongruous. They cannot easily exist side-by-side because each by nature is exclusive.

Self-centered self-love is so powerful, so ingrained that it controls us exclusively. We know we must surrender the immoral egoistic motive to the higher motive of loving God. But we cannot love God enough to supplant the self-centered love simply because we love self too much to allow a place for God-centered love.

Quite obviously we need divine help, and this is the function of the Holy Spirit. Initially we may be unwilling for the center of gravity in our lives to shift from self to Christ, but we must be willing to be *made* willing. Then the Spirit of God can motivate us toward the new motive.

We cannot expect to be "zapped" by a new motive, as if we are helpless victims of our desires. We can choose the desires we respond to. Love is more moral than sentimental; it is a disposition we can choose to have. The Holy Spirit has already kindled in our hearts at least a flickering love-flame for Christ. Now we must fan the flame and fuel it.

One secret is to get to know Jesus Christ in a spiritually intimate way, for to know Him is to love Him. The desire to please Christ is born in our relationship to Him. In that new relationship the old self-centered life is more easily surrendered, the selfishness crucified, the exorbitant self-love replaced with love for Him. To some people, knowing Christ intimately sounds too abstract to handle, but the human spirit is equipped with such possibilities and the Spirit of God gives special assistance. Christ can come alive as a real person in the inner sanctuary of the human soul.

Because this love motive emerges from a growing relationship, it is often too much to expect a new Christian to be controlled by love for Christ. The notion of a "second experience" does not describe God's arbitrary formula as much as it describes human personality. It is *descriptive* rather than *prescriptive*. The need for a deeper working of God's grace does not indicate inadequacy of God's initial grace. It simply reflects the inability of the human personality to entertain an adequate love motive for Christ until His fellowship has been consistently shared.

In this interpersonal relationship, which often seems too secret to express, the love motive is born. In Martin Buber's classic phrase, it is an "I-Thou encounter," not an "I-Thee encounter." That is to say, it is not a subject-object relationship as much as a subject-subject interrelationship. It is reciprocal. The love moves in both directions making it intimate and intense, the kind of love that exists within the Trinity itself.

Entering into this tender relationship presupposes a surrender of the despotic self-love that would sabotage it. As the old motive is surrendered, the new is established; as the new gains privilege, the old loses control. Christ becomes both the object and the subject of an affection that is at once liberating and enslaving.

Lifestyle of love

Before I suggest what sanctification is not, I must strongly assert its radical nature to the contemporary mind-set. A lifestyle motivated by love for Christ is foreign to a large portion of Western Christians for whom Christian faith is little more than a shock absorber in life, a special coupon to cash in when resources are limited or a ticket to heaven.

In our society we speak of love so freely that we easily forget the high cost of loving. Being motivated by love for Christ means a lifestyle of abandonment to our relationship with Christ. In loving, we do not *give love* — we *give ourselves*. Love is not a gift *from* the giver; it is a gift *of* the giver. In loving we commit ourselves to a relationship. In that relationship is generated the motivational force that brings our lives under its sway.

I am not suggesting that others should feel the particular feelings I experienced in the college grove. The essential elements are surrender and the implantation of a love motive strong enough to supplant the self motive. It means a person is willing to "go for broke."

The surrender I have spoken of is not an acquiescent submission, but a real desire, a delight to please Him. Love is dynamic, not passive. It is motivational, not suppressive. A cue comes from Psalm 40:8: "I desire to do your will, O my God; / your law is within my heart."

Like the ideal Christian marriage, this love relationship with Christ is so full and rich that surrendering the other relationships is not even considered a sacrifice.

A love desire to please Christ is not something extra for the Christian. It is basic to Christian sanctity. It is not a dessert, but the main course — not a sideshow, but the main tent. It is not a motive to which we can resort to when convenient; it is a controlling force to which we have committed our lives. We have abandoned everything else. In time, applause and pleas of the world have a hollow ring. We are marching to a different drumbeat. His smile is singularly our greatest delight! This is the lifestyle of love.

When I was in seminary my dad wrote these words to me: "The most glorious calling in all the world is the call to represent Christ, to stand for Him, to fight for Him, and to die for Him. Whether we live or die, it is unto Him, the fullness of All in All."

Many years ago F. Brook wrote:

> My goal is God Himself—not joy, nor peace,
> Nor even blessing, but Himself, my God.
> 'Tis His to lead me there, not mine, but His—
> "At any cost, dear Lord, by any road!"
>
> One thing I know, I cannot say Him nay;
> One thing I do, I press towards my Lord;
> My God my glory here from day to day,
> And in the glory there my Great Reward.[2]

Conflicting Motives

SURELY I WAS NOT SO NAIVE as to think my life from this point on would run smoothly. The opposite in fact seemed true. All sorts of competition developed. Opposing motives lifted their heads. Battles raged. The conflict was not between the outside war and me—it was civil war, between conflicting motives within. My forces were divided; I struggled with myself.

If my new motive experience was sanctification, I thought I would have no further inner conflict, only external. I was supposed to be free from that old two-word phrase so central to doctrinal disagreements—"carnal nature." But it was not quite so simple.

Discussing carnal nature is something we generally prefer to avoid. The problem is that foreign connotations have coagulated on the phrase, congesting its central meaning. Ordinarily we think of *carnal* as something physical, sensual or sexual. But in theology carnal nature generally refers to a particular *character disposition*—an innate, inborn, inbred tendency to sin. As a sin principle it is distinguished from a sin committed as a sinful condition is distinguished from a sinful act.

Carnal nature is inherited

According to historic theology, this sin principle is

27

acquired from committing sinful acts, but paradoxically sinful acts often spring from the sin principle. More than being acquired, therefore, a measure of this depravity is inherited — not genetically as I inherited my dad's big ears, but *anthropologically* as I would inherit my dad's estate even if I had been an adopted son. I inherit it *culturally* simply from being a part of the family. And rather than being inherited from one's immediate parents, carnal nature is inherited from the original progenitor of the human race, Adam. In this way carnal nature is a product of our being part of this morally wounded world.

Living in our kind of society and occupying our kind of bodies, we are obviously exposed to detrimental influences that do not originate in our character. The question then is this: *Where do I draw the line between those evil influences that originate in my moral nature and those that come from outside?* Often the two seem inextricably entangled. A temptation may originate in my character and be triggered by a television commercial. Or it may originate on Madison Avenue and find favorable response in my morally bent nature.

What many people have overlooked, and what I want to focus on in this chapter, is that *outside temptation may appeal to legitimate human desire*, desire that should not be considered evil. Being tempted includes both an attraction and an inner something that is attracted. The inner something is what the temptation appeals to. It may be broadly referred to as desire. In considering this, I will try to explain what carnal is not. Then, in chapter 5, we will look at what carnal nature is.

An often-made mistake is to consider any desire

that can be triggered by temptation to be evil by definition. The mistake comes in failing to distinguish between carnal desires and legitimate human desires. There are many desires to which temptation can appeal. Consequently, there will always be conflicting motives. To identify all such desire as carnally evil, however, is a great mistake.

I have discovered three primary areas of legitimate human desire from which conflicting motives arise, all of which can lead to sin. But none of them, standing alone, should be considered evil or immoral.

Physical desire

After I have finished a sumptuous beefsteak supper, one which my digestive system can barely handle, my hostess suggests raspberry pie a la mode. Three hours earlier eating the pie would have been perfectly OK, but now it would be gluttony. The appetite for the pie is no more evil now than it was midafternoon. The desire is biochemical in nature and should not be considered carnally evil.

Walking down the sidewalk my eye suddenly catches an attractive female form that triggers involuntary sexual desire, which is pure chemistry. To "lust after" the woman would be psychological entertainment of the desire, fantasizing the possibility of gratification—this is strongly condemned by Jesus. But the "lusting after" is quite different from the involuntary desire. One is carnal and immoral. The other standing alone is physiochemical.

After a hard day at the office I come home to find my wife also very tired and needing me to go immediately to the grocery store. My bones are aching with fatigue and I want to find a horizontal position.

But what I want to do is different from what I ought to do. Yesterday it was morally right to stretch out on the couch after work, but today it is wrong until I have done the errand. Am I to assume that the physical desire for rest was legitimate yesterday but carnal and evil today?

During Jesus' temptation in the wilderness, Satan tempted Him to turn stones to bread to satisfy His hunger. His hunger to which temptation appealed was not an evil desire. Being "tempted in every way, just as we are" (Hebrews 4:15), He obviously had sexual desire, yet He was "without sin."

The point is that it is logically possible for a person with a morally pure character to experience temptation. I have labored this point because so many people assume that being tempted indicates the presence of carnal nature. If this is true, then Christian sanctity is impossible as long as we live. But if Jesus was tempted without having a carnal nature, then we must look for some other way to define it.

Conditioned responses

There are still other legitimate desires to which temptation can appeal. These are "conditioned" responses, both physical and psychological.

An alcoholic has been "on the wagon" for 20 years, but still has the physical desire to drink. Of course, he wants not to drink more than he wants to drink, but the physical desire remains for temptation to appeal to. Earlier intemperance was evil, but having the desire now is simply biochemical. It is not carnally evil.

Susan possessed a nasty negative attitude. She snarled with cynicism, growled like a watchdog and dared anyone to offend her. Her personality was like a time bomb waiting to be detonated. Then Christ came into her life in a new way, and she had an immediate change of attitude. Her heart became sympathetic and her personality congenial. She never wished to be harsh or bitter again.

But one day outside pressures built up until she felt as if she was going to explode. Before she knew what was happening, the old sarcastic attitude erupted. Then she thought, "That is not the real person that I am now; that was the old me, the person I used to be."

The old negativism had become habitual as a personality pattern, but the substance of the negativism had been removed by her spiritual experience. The pattern remained, though; it had been emotionally conditioned.

Personality patterns

As a rule, *personality patterns are not removed by spiritual experience; they are replaced by practice over a period of time.* An unwillingness to attempt to overcome the old pattern may indicate the carnal selfish nature remains. And allowing the old pattern to erupt may be an act of sinning. The pattern may have been acquired in the first place from acts of sin. But the pattern itself is simply a conditioned emotional mode of response and does not necessarily indicate the presence of what we call carnal nature.

Similarly, John's carnal nature had conditioned his personality with patterns that expressed his arrogant, exaggerated self-centeredness. He had to tell the biggest story and get the best laugh. He exhausted freight-loads of energy jockeying for position in an endless game of one-upmanship. Ruthless toward others, he trampled on their feelings, putting them down in order to build himself up.

Then Jesus Christ radically transformed John's life. He became other-centered instead of self-centered, and he felt delivered from his old attitudes. So highly honored that God would stoop to live in his life, John felt no need to boast ever again. At his personality center he was profoundly humble.

Days later John found himself in a stressful social situation, and before he realized what he was doing, braggadocio erupted. For John the pretentious boast was now not the expression of an arrogance that characterized his heart. Rather it was the eruption of an old pattern that was momentarily unchecked. It was totally incongruous with his new humility. It did not reflect a substantive attitude; it simply indicated a conditioned pattern that needed correcting. It should not be considered carnal nature.

Behaviorists make a serious mistake when they read all behavior as nothing more than mechanical response to environmental stimuli. But thoughtless religionists make just as serious an error when all behavior is read as the exclusive product of moral intent without allowing for additional variables.

Joe had acquired deep feelings of inferiority, not severe enough to be a complex, but feelings of inadequacy that warped his self-image and strained his relationships. Then a dynamic encounter with God boosted his confidence. Joe now felt like somebody, so much so that he thought he would feel comfortable as a nobody in the world. He stood so tall in God's eyes that he thought he could never feel inferior again.

Then it happened. The old feelings cropped up and depressed his spirit. It did not indicate that his religious experience was superficial. It simply reflected the tenacity of conditioned emotional patterns.

Eruptions of old sub-Christian patterns should be fewer and farther between as a person grows in his or her walk with God. Eventually the outward life will come more and more into line with the new personality center. But the outward eruption of an old pattern does not necessarily reflect what is at the center of a person's heart.

Emotional desires

There are not only physical desires and conditioned personality patterns to which temptation can appeal. There are also legitimate human emotional desires that can be attracted to temptation.

Donna was born a normal human being, but early on she was deprived of the love that parents normally give their children. As a young adult, illicit love became attractive. She did not have the desire to do anything wrong, but she truly hungered for human love. Mistakenly, she felt that the only love available to her was illicit. Though it was a great temptation for Donna, it did not necessarily indicate carnal nature.

Sinful desire is moral in nature; Donna's desire was emotional. To yield to the temptation would be an immoral act that we call sinning, but the temptation itself does not indicate an immoral nature. The temptation appeals to emotional desires rather than evil ones.

Of course, temptation can appeal to both the evil

desires *and* the legitimate physical or emotional desires. Evil desires complicate the temptation experience and make it much more difficult to handle. But
the point here is that temptation itself does not necessarily imply the existence of carnal nature. Temptation can attract legitimate human desires, even in
the absence of carnally evil desire.

Tim has a psychological need for distinction, an
emotional desire for recognition. This desire is attracted to all sorts of temptations that promise gratification. It is so much like evil desire that the line
between the two is often fuzzy. At times Tim himself
does not know whether the temptation is appealing
to one or the other. But the two are categorically
distinct. Having the temptation does indicate there
is a responsive desire. But standing alone it does not
indicate carnal self-centeredness. At times the temptation to vanity appeals merely to a person's appropriate amoral emotional desire for distinction and
self-worth.

Misreading desire

But there is the danger of a person misreading all
evil desire as emotional desire, thus making inappropriate excuses for sinful actions. When this happens,
a person fails to recognize the need for divine grace
for spiritual emancipation from the carnal nature.

Likewise, there is the danger of mistaking legitimate emotional desires for carnal desires. The mistake creates feelings of guilt and an attitude of de-
featism, divesting a person of the moral victory that
he or she could otherwise experience.

Temptation can appeal to all sorts of legitimate
physical and emotional desires. Hunger can respond

to the temptation to gluttony. Appropriate sex drive can be attracted to immorality. Tiredness and desire for rest can respond to the temptation of laziness. Appropriate emotional desire for recognition can be attracted to arrogance. The legitimate human desire to love and be loved can respond to the temptation of exploitation.

In the next chapter we will define carnal nature in motivational terms. Here we have looked at some erroneous ideas of what the carnal nature is. If it is to be defined as any desire or condition to which temptation can appeal, obviously it can never be eliminated, and consequently what we call the holy heart is impossible. But if we distinguish between carnal nature and the legitimate physical and emotional desires of human nature, we may just discover that Calvary grace is adequate to conquer and cleanse the evil condition of the carnal heart.

This distinction was, for me, like an emancipation proclamation. Now I was freed from misconceptions that had sabotaged my pilgrimage. I could accept my conflicting motives as legitimate human desires, which required discipline, without feeling sinful for having the desires. I could now pursue my ideal of Christian sanctity realistically.

Illegitimate Motives

THE COLLEGE GROVE EXPERIENCE in no way eliminated my physical and emotional desires, nor
were my preconditioned personality patterns automatically restructured. These I consider neither
moral nor immoral, but morally legitimate for human beings with physical bodies and emotional
structures.

Conflict with these motives, however, was confusing, sometimes making me wonder whether they
actually controlled my life. At times these motives
were strong and the desires intense.

There was no denying that these fluctuating motives were near the surface of my life, but I had
discovered for myself a deeper motive to please
Christ. This new motive was not always as intense as
the others, but it affected a deeper level of my spirit.
It was positioned for control. Intensity would be a
matter of cultivation.

Surface desires would remain, but a profound
change had taken place at the center of my life. The
craving to satisfy the surface desires had been replaced by a longing to please Christ. Inside I was
more pleased from pleasing Him than I was from
pleasing myself. Earlier I had felt a deep yearning to

satisfy all my desires. Now that was being dissolved in my new motive.

Surface desires lost priority. For years, since birth really, they had been fueled and fired by the deep urge to gratify them. Now they were controllable. The deeper motive centered on another object, an object far enough beyond myself to free me from myself. That object was a Person.

Until we recognize the distinction between surface motives (physical and emotional) and in-depth motives (moral and spiritual), we cannot understand what I consider to be an appropriate notion of sanctification. If the deep motive is simply to satisfy the shallow desires, it is evil and carnal. If it is a love motive to please Christ, it is holy and good. Figures 1 and 2 illustrate this difference.

The object of sanctification is not to eliminate all conflicting motives or struggles with temptation — ultimately that would mean abolishing legitimate human desires. The object is to eliminate the deep-level immoral motive to satisfy self — what I call carnal nature — by replacing it with the motive to please Christ.

What has been called carnal nature is not something with spatial dimensions that can be eradicated by radical surgery or specific acts. It is more like a particular mind-set, a character condition, a moral warp or twist of a person's nature. Carnal nature is the nature to indulge the carnal. The carnal mind is the mindedness to satisfy surface desires. It is the deep-level personality motive to satisfy legitimate human desires without consideration for what is right. It is the yearning to gratify desires even when the gratification is morally dubious and involves sacrific-

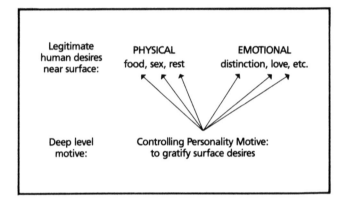

Figure 1.

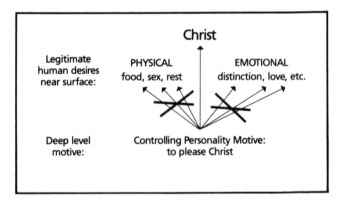

Figure 2.

ing moral rightness. It is the motive to place priority on the surface desires, to please oneself above pleasing God.

To explain further, it is being driven by self-centeredness. What is called carnal nature is subconscious selfishness. It is a motive that saturates one's very nature, cramping and hampering it, warping and twisting it, bending it toward oneself, preventing it from being straight toward God. It is an immoral motive that drives one ruthlessly, enslaving the selfhood, sabotaging moral and spiritual hopes, intentions and dreams.

Sanctification

The object of sanctification, then, is to install a new motive, one that is strong enough to preempt the immoral craving to satisfy the surface motives when they are attracted to temptation. This new motive is a motive beyond the other human motives of life. It creates an inner spiritual climate in which the chaos of motivation can be simplified.

It is moral in the sense that it is a desire to direct other motives to rightness and goodness. It provides resources for times of temptation.

To have this motive is to have a condition of Christian sanctity, but it does not mean a person will automatically live a life of sanctity. A condition of sanctity logically precedes a life of sanctity, but the second does not follow mechanically from the first. There are additional variables in the formula. Preconditioned personality patterns, habits or weaknesses often obstruct the practical flow of life from the condition of the heart. To have this motive, however, does mean that one has the desire and the intent to live out a life of sanctity.

So far I have broadly defined the positive ingredient of sanctification as the installation of a new motive. But sanctification is as much a negative term as a positive one, expressing the *absence* of certain things, not just an additional ingredient. We often think of the terms purity and cleanliness as if they were positive, but they are really negative in that they express the absence of defilement, pollution or corruption. Likewise, sanctification is more than the installation of a new motive by the Spirit of God; it is the replacement of an old motive with a new one. It eliminates a bad by depositing a good. Again, the old bad motive that needs replacing is what we call carnal nature.

Self-love

When we consider carnal nature and sanctification, we necessarily have to look at the terms *self-love* and *self-crucifixion*. Whether to love or to hate oneself is a controversy that goes back at least as far as Aristotle.[3]

In our day organic evolution has stripped human beings of feelings of purpose behind life. B.F. Skinner compounded the problem by reducing people to robots who are mechanically manipulated by environmental stimuli. Consequently, we feel divested of value and self-esteem, and we often look at ourselves with great disdain.

One reaction against this thinking is Robert Schuller's provocative books, *Self-Love: The Dynamic Force of Success* and *Self-Esteem: The New Reformation*.

John R.W. Stott puts the problem in perspective

by distinguishing between what people are by creation and what they are by the Fall. By creation and redemption we are good, dignified and noble; by the Fall we are bad, depraved and ignoble. The one should be highly esteemed and the other strongly rebuked.[4]

David K. Clark makes a valid distinction between being worthy and having worth. Self-esteem based on the second should be affirmed, while self-love based on the first should be prohibited.[5] C.S. Lewis suggests that we should love ourselves "with charity instead of partiality."[6]

I have defined carnal nature as the sinful motive to place human desires above both moral oughtness and the desire to please God. It is selfish, egocentric self-love rather than healthy self-esteem. It is partiality rather than charity toward self. It is the kind of pride that is opposite humility rather than a pride that is opposite shame.

Inadequate self-esteem results in a lack of confidence, even to the point of hating oneself and becoming masochistic. Healthy self-esteem enables a person to accept and live comfortably with himself or herself and to relate easily with others.

There may also be such a thing as excessive self-esteem, which results in arrogance and narcissism. It is an obsession with oneself that preempts meaningful relationships with God and with other people. Here it becomes a moral problem. It is self-centered self-love, and it cannot be confused with having a healthy self-image.

Carnal nature, however, does not always focus on excess self-esteem, and therefore it is not always expressed in arrogance. Sometimes it focuses on excess

"sense-esteem," expressing itself in physical indul-
gences such as gluttony, laziness or immoral sex.
Here a person, like an animal, identifies the self
with the physical senses. Self becomes subservient to
physical desires.

Refining the definition

Let us refine the definition of carnal nature still
further. Carnal nature should not be defined as appropriate consideration or appreciation for oneself.
Instead it is a consideration for oneself that supersedes and deactivates a functional love for Christ. It
is the area of self-love that goes beyond one's love for
God, the kind of self-love that supplants and dimin-
ishes God-love. It is not the desire to please oneself,
but the *excessive* desire to please oneself, the desire
to please self more than God. It is not the motive to
gratify desire, but the exaggerated, blown-up motive
to satisfy desire — the motive to do so at the expense
of not satisfying Christ. It is being more pleased by
pleasing self than by pleasing God.

Self-crucifixion

Down through the years theologians have often
expressed the idea that the self is bad and that it
must be "crucified." I can accept the notion with the
understanding that language is imprecise and often
not capable of communicating specific implications
accurately. What the phrase is getting at is com-
mendable, though confusing. It seems to castigate
the self as if it were inherently and metaphysically
bad and should not be allowed to survive. But this
conflicts with the worthy notion of self-esteem and a
positive, healthy self-image.

If the self is so hopelessly bad that it deserves crucifixion, it seems to me that we have no excuse for existence, and that all attempts at survival are evil.

A correct position is somewhere between the two extremes of self-hatred and self-indulgence. The New Testament implicitly teaches positive self-regard and explicitly teaches self-denial. But I do not interpret "take up your cross" and "crucify the flesh" as commands to crucify the self. Taking up the cross means a willingness to be crucified, not self-crucifixion. The self is not metaphysically bad; it is morally bad. It does not need to be destroyed—its badness needs to be destroyed so that the self can become morally good. "Crucifying the flesh" suggests the destruction of the "motive beyond the motives," the swollen selfish desire to please self.

Ego and egotism

Another way of looking at the distinction is to note the difference between ego and egotism. The term ego is incorrectly used to mean egotism. Actually, ego simply refers to the self—the thinking and feeling, self-conscious self.

What needs eliminating is not the self/ego, but the selfishness/egotism that accumulates around the self, the self-centeredness that smothers and strangles it. The self needs to be liberated from the selfishness, the ego from the egotism. Selfishness and egotism need to be stripped away, eliminated, "crucified" so that the personality, the ego-self, can be free. The self needs to be emancipated from what Dennis Kinlaw calls "the tyranny of self-interest."[7]

This selfishness is the "motive beyond the motives," the immoral desire beyond the human desires.

It is what I have called carnal nature. The "crucifying" of that selfishness is the replacing of that immoral motive with a moral motive to please Christ. It is what I have called sanctification. It results in what we call a holy heart.

With this desire to please Christ more than self, we can be "crucified with Christ" (Romans 6:6, 11) while hardly being aware of it. We are more preoccupied with Him than we are with ourselves. Consequently we can have a martyr's spirit without having a martyr's complex.

Correct definitions

I have attempted to explain, from several angles, what I mean by carnal nature and sanctification. Correct definitions are important to correct understanding. If we define carnal nature as any legitimate human desire to which temptation can appeal, then it cannot be eliminated. Similarly, if we define sanctification as the crucifixion of the legitimate human self with its human desires, then it can never occur. But if we define carnal nature as I have, as the immoral motive behind human desires, then I can see no reason why it cannot be replaced with Christian sanctity.

Eradication of controversy

Before I leave this chapter, I want to take time to look at a controversy that has sprung up around two terms. Some sanctificationists argue over whether sanctification is eradication of carnal nature or a redirecting of the will. Quite frankly, I do not see the point of the controversy. Both notions employ models that lend themselves to spatial dimensions.

What we are talking about, however, is not spatial in nature. Neither model, therefore, can be pushed too far. But either can be used if its limitations are understood.

The word *eradication* suggests taking something out of something else and putting it in another place. The term is used in Matthew 15:13, not specifically in relationship to sanctification, and is translated in the Authorized Version as "rooted up." The eradication analogy is inappropriate to sanctification if carried too far, because carnal nature is not something substantive that can be dug up and deposited in some other place. But if the word is used to mean the replacing of a self-centered character motive with a love motive to please Christ, then it may be workable.

The idea of redirecting or straightening the will is also a metaphor with spatial implications. The idea here is that a person's will is bent toward self and needs to be straightened toward God. The bend in the will is defined as carnal nature, and the straightening of the will is sanctification. Of course, when the will is straightened the bend is eliminated, not in the sense that it is deposited in some other place, but eliminated just the same. An evil motive has been replaced by a higher motive.

Cleansing is another word often used in reference to carnality. This is a model that conjures in our minds certain pictures of water and detergent that are inappropriate to the experience of sanctification. But the model can be appropriately used if it is understood to be symbolic.

Sometimes I use the term *dissolve,* in the sense that the old motive (carnal nature) is dissolved in the new (sanctification). This is also a figure of speech, attempting to get at what happens rather than to state it precisely.

Perhaps the term *replacement* carries less unusable baggage than some of the other terms. The carnal desire to please self is replaced with the holy desire to please Christ.

CHAPTER
6

Keeping It
in Perspective

WITHOUT MUCH EFFORT, someone could take what
I have said and "run out of the ball park with it."
But the pleasing-Christ motive needs to be kept in
perspective. In this chapter I am suggesting two distinctions that should further refine the notion and
structure it for practical serviceability.

The motive and its object

First, there is a difference between the motive and
its object, between the *desire* to please Christ and
pleasing Christ. Placing priority on having the motive can obscure the object of the motive.

When my children were small, they had a standard
alibi: "I didn't mean to." We all know people who
excuse their wrong actions on the grounds that they
had the right motives. But having right motives is
not enough. To be effective the motives have to
result in appropriate action.

This is especially true when we consider sanctification. As much as the motive or the desire does for
us, it is not an end in itself. The object of the motive
is to please Christ, not just to have the motive—
otherwise any motive would do. When the desire
becomes an end in itself, it gets turned in on itself

47

and becomes a motive to have the motive. Eventually it will dissipate.

When I look inside my consciousness to discover the motive, I sometimes have difficulty finding it. But when I think of pleasing Christ, with emphasis on Christ, the motive reappears. The desire remains intact as long as I keep looking at the object of the desire.

It is similar to the love between a husband and wife. If a husband looks within himself, he may feel barren, impoverished, emotionally empty. But when he looks at his wife, he discovers love — not something static within but something focused on the one loved. His love for his wife grows and matures, not by taking his emotional temperature but by his concentration on his wife. The object of his love becomes the subject, being in a sense the very source of his love.

To reiterate, the danger is in becoming preoccupied with the desire rather than with pleasing Christ. The desire cannot exist of itself. Its existence is derived from its object. When the focus is on the desire, it has a tendency to evaporate. Though sanctification may center in the desire, the desire must focus on Christ.

Christian sanctification is not just a deposited love; it is loving God. It is not just a controlling motive, but a motive to please Christ. It is not just a desire that liberates from lesser desires; it is a desire that liberates by enslaving a person to the highest value. The focus is on Christ.

Pleasing and satisfying

A second distinction is between pleasing Christ

and satisfying Him. I was highly pleased when my five-year-old son learned to read *cat* and *rat* and *dog*. I was pleased that as a seven-year-old he read scores of 200-page books in their entirety. But I will not be satisfied with his reading until he gets off Trixie Belden, Berenstain Bears and Sunday comics and is reading Plato and Aristotle, Augustine and Aquinas, Shakespeare, Emerson and Thoreau. C.S. Lewis quotes George MacDonald as saying, "God is easy to please, but hard to satisfy."[8] This distinction is important, specifically for preventing problems in four areas.

First, without the constant challenge of satisfying Christ with our lives, there is danger of *complacency* from knowing He is pleased with our motive. Feeling smug from pleasing Him, we would become self-satisfied and never activate the motive in a practical way.

One of my students completely misread my compliment early on in one course. After learning that his initial paper had pleased me, he falsely assumed that he had satisfied the course requirements for the full semester. He thought he was home free. I was pleased with his progress to that point, but in no way would I be satisfied until he passed the final. Coasting through the rest of the course was not an option.

No place in these chapters have I said that we can completely satisfy Christ. He will not be satisfied with us until we are emancipated from every personality pattern that binds us, every emotional hang up, every damaged feeling, every poorly placed priority, every inconsistency, every moral weakness. He will not be satisfied until we are rid of every personality quirk, every eccentricity, every irregularity of thought and feeling. We have a long distance to go. The journey is never complete on earth. Stronger character is yet to be built, higher maturity to be reached, greater sympathies to be developed. Robert Browning wrote: "Ah, but a man's reach should exceed his grasp, or what's a heaven for?"[9]

Second, without realizing that we never completely satisfy Him, there is danger of *narcissism* — inordinate self-esteem, even self-praise. We pat ourselves on the back for having the motive to please Him, congratulating ourselves that we have arrived at such an admirable position. We can even come to believe that we deserve God's favor. By simply having the motive to please Him, we think we have made points with God. Without even realizing it, we start using our "spiritual" position as a coupon for special privileges.

Of course, as soon as we feel the self-praise we lose the motive to please Christ. It is replaced with the motive to please ourselves.

The strongest, purest and safest self-esteem is not from what we are or what we have done. It is from feeling the distinction of being recognized by God, from knowing we are important to Him, from the value He places on us. We should feel as if we were on a marked-down counter in the bargain basement and Jesus Christ came along and put an infinite price tag on us. Our self-esteem is bestowed, not earned. It is given, not deserved.

We did not even have the creative power to generate our own motive to please Him. We did choose it, but only after it was offered to us by the Holy Spirit. Now that we have the motive, which pleases Christ, we are still far short of our ideal of satisfying Him. Making the distinction is humbling.

False guilt

Third, without realizing the difference between pleasing Christ and satisfying Him, there is the danger of *false guilt*. This was one of my problems during high school and college. Unable to satisfy Christ completely, I simply assumed that He was displeased with me.

Without making this distinction the standard seems so high that we cannot possibly measure up. Then false guilt arises. This guilt in turn creates a problem for the motive to please Him. The guilt tempts us to use the motive as a tool to absolve the guilt, as a reparation payment.

When this happens the motive to please Christ is not for the sake of pleasing Christ but for emotional cleansing from guilt. Then it is distorted; it loses its purity. It is not a motive to please Christ at all, but a motive to use pleasing Christ as a sponge to absorb the guilt. A lesser motive has usurped the higher while pretending to be the higher.

Distinguishing between pleasing Christ and satisfying Christ allows us to live within our own boundaries without feeling guilty. The motive to please Christ is freed up from a strangling guilt so that it can work toward satisfying Christ in a positive way.

Fourth, without realizing the difference between pleasing Christ and satisfying Him, there is the danger of *remaining unsettled* in our position. Expecting Him to be displeased until He is satisfied, we are unable to relax in our desire to please Him or to be settled in it and resting on it. We have no joy in our attempts to satisfy Him, no buoyancy of spirit. Living under a divine frown, we miss the therapy of His smile. We feel dissonant with heavenly music, out of harmony with universal order. The Christian life becomes a burden.

Being a fourth generation preacher, I have had quite a heritage to live up to. I started preaching at age 16, often with my father in the congregation. As I look back to that time, I realize there was no way he could have been satisfied with my preaching — not with the degree of professionalism he had. Yet never once did he fail to let me know how pleased he was with my efforts.

Our motive pleases God

It is almost beyond our capacity to think: God does not wait until He is satisfied with us to be pleased with us. He actually allows Himself to enjoy pleasure from our desire to satisfy Him. It is our motive to please Him that pleases Him.

A heart condition of Christian sanctification has to do with the desire and intent to please Him, while the life of Christian holiness has to do with attempts to satisfy Him.

Understanding He is pleased with our love-desire to please Him, we can be settled in that motive and can experience the peace that comes in knowing He has allowed Himself to be pleased with us! The good news is that we do not have to wait until we totally satisfy Christ to contribute to His pleasure and His eternal glory!

Plugging in Theological Jargon

"**D**ON'T TALK THEOLOGY TO ME," says the pragmatist. "Give me something practical." The not-so-opaque implication is that theology by its nature is unrelated to life.

Most of us have little interest in playing semantic games with esoteric language understood only by the initiated few. Pure theory with no applicability has little appeal and even less value. Before going on, then, to what may have more practical appeal, we must deal with some rather common theological phrases and try to understood them in a practical way.

A work of grace

Some people contend that sanctification should be considered as a "work of grace," by which they generally mean something comparable in gravity and magnitude to personal salvation. My initial question is whether salvation here refers to being rescued from hell or salvaged from sin (including selfishness, a meaningless life and so on).

Broadly, everything God does to move us away from sin, selfishness and hell toward goodness, sanctity and heaven is a product of grace. Every step in our pilgrimage away from a dark past toward a bright future is the activity of God's grace. That grace was "at work" in our lives before we ever knew Christ, and it is "working" in our lives every hour.

Sanctification, as I have defined it, is not simply switching from one motive to another. It is switching from a selfish motive to a God-centered one, replacing a bad motive with a good one. Hence sanctification *is* a moral operation beyond a person's own ability to perform — a "work of God's grace."

The selfish motive is just as much a *condition* of sin as telling a lie is an *act* of sin. And cleansing a condition of sin is no less a work of special grace than forgiving an act of sin. If justification is a product of grace, so is sanctification. Calvary grace has provided a basis upon which human beings can be both forgiven of sins committed and cleansed from sinful motives. God's work in our lives includes both a forgiven past and a changed future. Sanctification must never be thought of as only a psychological gimmick to free people from selfish motives. The selfish motive is a condition of sin, the elimination of which is the function of divine grace.

Christian perfection

Perfection talk "is not idealistic gas," C.S. Lewis said.[10] We shy away from discussing perfection, partly because we wish to be humble, but also because we do not want the challenge of so high a standard. Complacency is more convenient, and mediocrity more comfortable. By ridiculing the notion of perfection we wedge out elbow room for a sub-Christian lifestyle. It has even become popular to boast about our "human imperfections," often under the guise of humility, as if we become more holy by bragging about our sins.

Yet we cannot shake loose from those disturbing words of Jesus: "Be perfect" (Matthew 5:48). The voice of God rolls like thunder in Genesis 17:1 (KJV): "I am the almighty God; walk before me, and be thou perfect." Again Scripture says, "Thou shalt be perfect with the Lord thy God" (Deuteronomy 18:13, KJV), and again, "Be perfect" (2 Corinthians 13:11, KJV).

Obviously there are many senses in which we can never be perfect, but these must not eclipse the sense in which we are expected to be perfect. Because perfection is an absolute term, there can be no comparative or superlative degrees of perfection. Something cannot be more perfect or less perfect, most perfect or least perfect. It is either perfect or imperfect. But *perfection is only absolute in the area to which the perfection refers.*

For example, a drinking glass can be perfectly full without being perfectly empty. A dish can be perfectly clean without being perfectly round. There is a difference between perfect action and perfect attitude. One may be legally at fault without being morally to blame. It is possible to be morally clean without being morally strong. One may have perfect love without being a perfect lover. Perfect purity does not necessarily mean perfect maturity. We may have perfect intentions and imperfect actions.

So what is the area of perfection that is expected of us as Christians? Without minimizing the importance of Christian action, the commandment is to *be* perfect rather than to *do* perfectly. It seems to refer to a condition, a disposition, a character state, an attitude, a controlling motive rather than a perfection of outward human action. It comes close to being what I have described as an unselfish love relationship with Christ, desiring to please Him more than ourselves.

John Wesley clarified his view of Christian perfection as follows:

> "Sinless perfection" is a phrase I never use.
>
> What is implied by being a perfect Christian? The loving of God with all our heart, and mind, and soul.
>
> [Christian perfection] is purity of intention; . . . it is one desire and design ruling all our tempers; . . . it is the loving of God with all our heart.[11]

It is important to note, however, that the commandment is to "love the Lord your God with all *your* heart"—not with all the pope's heart or the pastor's heart. Your heart may not be as large as someone else's; it may not have the capacity for love that another has. But if you love with all *your* heart, the love is unthreatened. For you, it is perfect love.

More important, it is qualitative love rather than quantitative. There is always room for the love to grow in volume, because a person's heart always has room to expand. As the heart enlarges, its capacity for greater love increases. But the greater volume of love is not qualitatively superior to the lesser love, if both come from undivided hearts. A teacup of water is less than one-sixteenth as much as a gallon, but it can be just as good, just as pure, just as hot—it can be precisely the same quality as the other.

Process or crisis

The sometimes fiery controversy over whether sanctification is a process or an instantaneous crisis experience does not need to be refueled here. Rather I want my discussion to be an attempt at reconciling the two factions.

Wesley himself never claimed that sanctification is exclusively a crisis experience. According to Wesley, from the moment a person is saved, he or she "gradually dies to sin, and grows in grace."[12] Most reputable Wesleyan theologians have recognized the place of the process to the point that they have distinguished between "initial" sanctification — what occurs at conversion — and "entire" sanctification — what happens at a later time. Those who claim that sanctification is exclusively a "second blessing" are more "Wesleyan" than Wesley himself. They are not in the mainstream of Wesleyan theology.

The real disagreement rides on the issue of "entire" sanctification. And the answer turns on one's definition of carnal nature and sanctification.

If carnal nature is defined as temptation appeal or as human physical and emotional appetites, then it can never on earth be completely eliminated, and entire sanctification is impossible. But there are two problems with this definition. First, it means Jesus had a carnal nature, and second, it means God's special grace is inadequate to restore man from moral depravity. The Cross then is not curative; it merely bandages sores that we must carry through life. The death of Christ is only a stopgap measure until eternity can do its work.

But if carnal nature is defined as I have defined it — as a deep motive to make oneself central in life, an immoral motive beyond the legitimate human motives—then certainly God's grace is adequate to cleanse, shift or replace the carnal nature with a motive to please Christ. If this motive to please Christ is acquired and remains in place, then the Christian is in a state of sanctity.

This in no way means the Christian lives a life of complete sanctity, for there are variables in the transition formula from what a person is to what a person does. And it in no way means that a person has arrived at maturity or perfection in living out the life of Christian holiness. The need to reach higher, push forward and "press toward the mark" is never eliminated. But it does mean the Christian has arrived at a certain milestone in his or her sojourn with Christ. It is a landmark of complete surrender and a shift of motive from self to Christ.

A "crisis" in two senses

Now back to the question. One does not generally occupy this new position in life by one big crisis leap. The *pilgrimage* is a process. But the *arrival* is a "crisis" in two senses.

First, it happens at a point in time. Two days ago I may have been nine-tenths surrendered, but now I am fully surrendered. When I surrendered the last beachhead, I entered a new category. Earlier I was not totally surrendered. Now I am. There came a time in the long process when I crossed over the line. In that sense it is a crisis.

Second, it is a crisis in the sense that my relationship with myself and with Christ is changed. I experience a new freedom from myself that I could not possibly experience so long as a residual self-serving motive enslaved me. And I have a new freedom in my love-service for Christ since this old preemptive motive is replaced.

My 700-mile trip home was a long trek. Each mile brought me closer, and with each mile came greater excitement. With only one mile to go, my relationship with my family was the same as when I began the journey home—absent husband and daddy-away-from-home. But when I crossed the threshold into our home, my relationship with my family shifted from daddy-away to daddy-at-home. Every mile I motored was necessary to get home, but only the last step changed my status from away to at-home.

My journey toward full surrender to Christ was a necessary process. But at 99 percent surrender, my status with Christ was that of a not-fully-surrendered Christian, the same as at 10 percent surrender. When I reached 100 percent surrender, though, my relationship with Christ shifted to that of a fully surrendered Christian. (See Figure 3.)

Just as the final step into my home was for me more dramatic than any one of the other 700 miles I crossed earlier, that last percent surrender was more radically unsparing than any of the earlier necessary surrenders I had made.

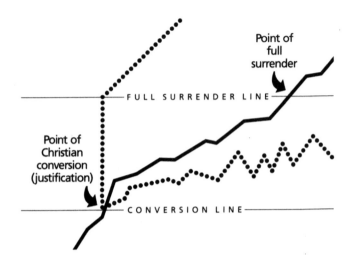

Figure 3. Uneven line maps a person's spiritual journey. The person begins (bottom left) as unregenerate. Instead of immediate conversion, there is usually a progressive positive attitude toward God (period of awakening). Though the journey is a process, the line is crossed into the kingdom of God at a point in time.

Theoretically a person could immediately enter the full release of completely surrendered motives (vertical dotted line), but in practice few do so. The growth is uneven, not smooth, but it is consistently upward. Some never reach the Spirit-controlled line, continuing to wander in the wilderness of self-centered motives (uneven dotted line).

When a person crosses the full surrender line, a new freedom and power is released. Desire to please Christ moves to center stage and becomes the operating base. Though it is ordinarily only one step in a continuing journey, surrender of the last residual unsurrendered motive occurs at a point in time. One may not recognize its import, considering it only another step in the progression. But it is a radical step in that one moves into *full* surrender, a position that allows the Spirit of God new freedom to function in one's life. Though a landmark has been reached, the pilgrimage continues and the growth process must not cease.

Filled with the Spirit

WHAT I EXPERIENCED IN THE COLLEGE GROVE was something beyond what I could accomplish. My noblest efforts at a sanctified life had been futile.

My new motive to please Christ obviously came from transcendent resources—I could not originate it. It was not mine, yet it was—not as my own creation, but as a gift. I owned the motive, not as its author, but as its recipient.

It was as if I were occupied by a force from another world. But I soon discovered that it was more than occupation. My personality was united, almost fused, with another Personality—one brighter, gentler and nobler than mine. Rather than shifting my inner self off base, as might be expected, the new Personality added cohesiveness and integration, making me more at home with myself.

It was a Personality I had long known as a Christian, but now the presence seemed more accessible, more intimate to my spirit. The divine Personality occupied my human personality. The infinite Spirit of God had homesteaded my finite human spirit.

The Apostle Paul wrote to the Ephesians, "Be filled with the Spirit" (Ephesians 5:18). Because of what is called the "continuing" present tense of the Greek verb, some have translated the clause: "Be *being* filled with the Spirit." From this has come the misinterpretation: "Be in a continuing process of becoming filled with the Spirit." A more accurate grammatical reading of the line, however, would be something like this: "Be in a continuing *state* of being *full* of the Spirit"—a state of being rather than a process of becoming.

Additionally, the phrase "filled with the Spirit" is a metaphor; the term *filled* is used as a spatial analogy. But here we are talking about something that is not spatial. If you push the term literally, the Holy Spirit is reduced to material substance measurable in cubic inches or centimeters. Human beings become passive receptacles.

When the term *filled* is applied to human personality, it generally means something like "occupied with," "controlled by" or "united with." Human personality is responsive to outside influence and control to the point that the outside force is "internalized" and "inhabits" a person's inner self.

My experience in the college grove was not an end in itself, but rather a kickoff for a new kind of living. God's Spirit was releasing me from enslaving self-serving motives. In so doing, He Himself was being freed from my restrictions on Him. I began to discover three ways the Holy Spirit is free to function in the life He occupies.

Intensified presence

First, the Holy Spirit brings a greater sense of divine presence. The human personality not only internalizes outside influence, it has been built to entertain another Personality. It is at home as host or hostess to a special Guest. It has been constructed with a capacity for divine occupancy.

This coalescence does not result in a loss of individual distinction and self-awareness. It is not a holistic oneness of substance. Rather it is a love-oneness of spiritual intimacy and personal accessibility. Speaking in the context of giving His Holy Spirit to Christians, Jesus said, "If anyone loves me . . . we will come to him and make our home with him" (John 14:23).

Can you imagine how the disciples felt when Jesus announced He was going to leave? They had been fired with His zeal and had committed their lives to Him. Then He announced He was going away. Surely their consternation was complicated when He said, "It is *for your good* that I am going away" (John 16:7). Then He explained that He would send the Holy Spirit to live with them.

What many have overlooked is that the Holy Spirit is Christ's Spirit. His presence brings Christ's presence. Jesus said, "The Spirit . . . will testify about me" (John 15:26), and "He will bring glory to me" (John 16:14).

For the disciples, what happened at Pentecost was something like the internalization of the external Christ. They had known Him in the flesh; now they knew Him in the Spirit. We have evidence that they knew Him much more closely after He ascended than while He walked among them. The Holy Spirit made the presence of Christ intimate to their spirits.

Deeper purity

A second function of the Holy Spirit is to produce moral purity on a deeper level. In justification (at

conversion) the Spirit appropriates pardoning grace
for committed sins. But in sanctification He appropriates cleansing, purifying grace for the condition
of sin — what I have called the motive to please self.

The phrase "filled with the Spirit" is used in more
than one way in the New Testament. At times it
refers to special spiritual anointing for ministry or
empowering for service. In Acts 2, however, the
phrase is synonymous with what Jesus called being
"baptized with the Holy Spirit" in Acts 1:5.

While the term *baptism* may have some controversial connotations, the word itself basically means
washing and cleansing. Water baptism is ceremonial,
symbolic cleansing, but "Spirit" baptism is moral and
spiritual cleansing.

No one can be cleansed from a selfish condition of
sin through human efforts. That is the Spirit's department. But He cannot cleanse us without our per-
mission. Surrendering to Him is our department.
Sanctification includes all we can do — surrender and
cooperate — and what God's Spirit alone can do —
purify and cleanse. The old selfish motive is replaced
by the new love motive. The human heart becomes
home for God's Spirit.

We are not filled with the Spirit primarily to make
temptation easier to handle or to eliminate the struggles inherent in Christian living. The highest purpose of the indwelling Spirit is Christian sanctity. He
wants to purify our motives and make us Christlike.

Greater power

Third, the Holy Spirit functions as energetic
power in the life He occupies. The power He provides is not emotionally explosive, dramatic or bois-

terous. Like some of the greatest natural forces on earth, it sometimes operates silently. Note how quietly gravity functions, and magnetism, and even electricity when it is under control. Our rooms are lighted, our homes heated and our meals cooked with astonishing silence. Elijah could not find the Lord in the wind or earthquake or fire — only in the "still small voice" (1 Kings 19:12, KJV).

These days we hear many Christians praying for power. Apparently some are praying for the strength to do something spectacular, something spiritually sensational. A self-centered Christian with such devious motives would use God's power for self-serving purposes. How defiling to oneself and dishonoring to God would be such self-glorification!

The primary power the Spirit gives us is the power to walk straight, to stand tall, to live right, to be good — the power to relate life situations to His adequacy! Standing alone, we are helpless. Sanctification, moral goodness and godliness are beyond our reach.

Since the primary purpose of God's power is moral, much of it flows into our lives indirectly from the Spirit, as a result of the deeper purity, the love motive to please God, the moral cleansing from self-centered motives.

Fully surrendered

Is every Christian filled with the Spirit? The answer is yes and no — without equivocating. Every Christian is filled with the Spirit *to the extent* that he or she is emptied of self and surrendered to Christ. No Christian is filled with the Spirit in the sense of being "full" until that person is fully surrendered in the area of his or her deepest motives. A person cannot be occupied with the presence of Christ so long as he or she is preoccupied with self.

It is the prerogative of every Christian to be filled. It is the responsibility of the Holy Spirit to do the filling. How can I be filled with the Spirit? It is not something I do — it is something I receive. There is no way I can *not* be filled with the Spirit — if I am totally surrendered and open to Him.

When this full surrender is in place and operating, the human personality can be inhabited by the personality of Christ. Saturated by His personality, we can know Him as a real Person. His presence is intensified. In Paul's words, we are "filled to the measure of all the fullness of God" (Ephesians 3:19).

Switching Over

ASSAULTED WITH TEMPTATION, our first inclination is to turn and run. But the temptation pursues us, outruns us, gets ahead of us, turns and stares us in the face. As we run from it, we run into it. There is a head-on collision.

The easiest way to handle temptation is to give in to it. But giving in is no solution. We have all heard the phrase, "I can resist everything but temptation."

Having the deep desire to please Christ gives us a base for resisting temptation. The love motive provides a beachhead for counterattack. Our reason for overcoming temptation is more than a principle—it springs from our relationship with a person, Jesus Christ.

Temptation is necessary

Though we would rather not fight the battle with temptation, we need it to provide an opportunity for us to function from our new motive. When life runs too easily or smoothly, we hardly know whether we are living by the new motive or by something else. Difficult life situations help us to confirm the deep motive, to activate it, to shift it into operating gear. We can only "practice" the new motive in practical situations. The desire to please Christ needs to be used, to be expressed, to be allowed to function. Unless we put it into practice, we have no way of knowing whether we really have it.

Therefore, when temptation is unavoidable, we should welcome it as an occasion to reconfirm our motive to please Christ. It is a select moment of great opportunity, a moment when we are at the moral heart of living.

Earlier I pointed out that having the deep motive to please Christ in no way precludes temptation's appeal to legitimate human desires. But the way of handling the temptation is changed.

No one has as much trouble with temptation as with the inner response to temptation. The evil suggestion does not grip a person—it is something in the person that latches onto the suggestion. We are not overcome by the temptation but by our own desires. The desires may be legitimate, not evil within themselves, but they grab hold of the evil suggestion and will not let it go. The person who operates from this desire base has no way to shake loose.

Surrendered Christians have already given these desires to Christ and are standing and living on a deeper desire to please Him. When they feel a certain desire beginning to respond to an evil suggestion, they "switch over" to the deeper desire. Now they are in a position to turn the temptation loose. They are not enslaved by the desire to which the suggestion has appealed.

Establishing the pattern

After I had succumbed to a persistent nemesis temptation, I looked back and recalled *not* having related the experience to my love for Christ and my desire to please Him. In the struggle of temptation, it never occurred to me to bank on my desire to please Him. Little wonder I collapsed.

Later on, after I had developed something of a pattern of switching over from self-desire to Christ-desire, I discovered it came more easily. The desire to please Christ, even when not in consciousness, was in the subconscious nearer the threshold of consciousness, easier to switch to.

But sometimes the self-desire surfaced, such as the time I became peeved at the NFL for scheduling the Superbowl on Sunday evening at the same time as church. I reluctantly went to church, but I was not happy about it.

A visiting speaker dragged the service out beyond an hour and a half, and my hopes of seeing any of the game were vanishing. After the speaker finished, the pastor got turned on, mercilessly exhorting on and on. My irritation grew by the minute.

When I finally got home, I discovered that it was only halftime and the score was nothing to nothing. I was relieved, but the relief was short-lived. The television cable suddenly went off and stayed off until just after the game ended! My wife said God might be trying to tell me something about my priorities. I preferred to blame it on the preacher and the cable company, neither of which would have received my vote in a popularity contest.

Before the TV came back on, I had finally switched over to my desire to please Christ. Tension and vexation evaporated, and I could relax at the center of my being. Now I had something to feel good about. I could still please Christ. Not even the long-winded preacher could prevent that. If I was to miss the entire game, so what? My life was still on course. I had something to rely on. Feeling good about Christ made me feel good about myself.

The Christian in whose heart Christ has deposited sanctity may spend a lifetime switching over — switching from the amoral human desires that respond to temptation to the deeper desire to contribute to the happiness and pleasure of Christ. The switching over should become habitual as the pattern is established more firmly. Some temptations that used to have such strong appeal lose their force as the surrendered Christian practices living from the deep motive.

Human desires

Here someone is apt to question why the committed Christian should ever need to "switch over." Returning to home base would never be necessary if a person never got off base in the first place.

The question exposes a misconception about human desires — that because they respond to temptation they are morally bad. If they were evil as supposed, certainly no one should ever venture close. But these desires, both physical and emotional, are distinctively human (as I have explained in earlier chapters). As such they are quite outside the moral categories of good and evil. They can be gratified immorally and lead to great evil, or they can be fulfilled appropriately for great good. The desire for food, for example, can lead either to gluttony or good health. Sexual desire can lead to debauchery or to legitimate expression of love. The emotional desire for distinction can lead to vanity or self-respect.

As human beings we have to live in a world where

these human desires are "out front." They are easily triggered by circumstances, both physical and social. Placating the desires within moral bounds is appropriate activity. If we were never to function on this level, we would end up being zombies—walking dead.

Because being human requires so much activity in the area of these human desires, we are "sitting ducks" for temptation. Living victoriously over temptation requires the deeper motive to hold the human desires in check. When there is strong appeal to one of these desires that could lead to sin, the surrendered Christian has a deeper desire to resort to the motive to please Christ.

For righteousness' sake is not enough

In times of temptation, I have discovered the principle of interpersonal motivation. For me it is easier to resist from my love for Christ than for righteousness' sake. Especially for the person whose character is not yet "firmed up" at the point of a particular temptation, the *oughtness* motive is often inadequate. I discover when I operate from oughtness alone that I am often "scrapping like mad" not to do what is not right. As soon as I switch my motive for doing right to a Person—pleasing Christ, for His sake—I can relax and surrender the temptation rather than having to fight against my own human desires.

Earlier I said the motive to please Christ dissipates when it becomes an end in itself and instead of looking to the desire we need to look to pleasing Christ. Nevertheless, in time of temptation it helps me to realize that pleasing Him is not only for His sake, but also *for my sake.* It is what I *want* to do. My desire is not different from His desire for me. While it is a desire to please *Him,* it is still *my* desire to please Him. I am not divided, forcing myself to do something I do not wish to do. I am integrated around the desire to please Him, doing what *I* desire, deeply pleasing myself by pleasing Him.

What every Christian needs for battling temptation is a selfless desire born out of a love-relationship with Christ. This love-relationship is fired by the motive to please Him, and it is strong enough to sustain an integrated personality while disciplining the human desires as a parent disciplines unruly children.

10

Other Temptations

"SWITCHING OVER" TO THE CHRIST-MOTIVE is applicable to every kind of temptation experience. Your experiences may be different from mine. So that I can better describe how "switching over" works, I will analyze some of my weaknesses.

Impatience

My work as a college professor and Christian minister requires that I use time wisely. Those people who are prompt, whose lives are scheduled and who learn to work comfortably within time structures are often accused of being robots, mechanically precise and impatient with those who are more freewheeling. I confess to the charge.

On the other hand, I consider those who are undisciplined by the clock slothful and indolent. Ordering one's life eliminates "spinning the wheels." Not only can more be accomplished, but there is also more time for guilt-free relaxation.

My propensity to budget time is probably less rigorous than it should be. But it is exacting enough to make me vulnerable to impatience with those persons who drift easily through the day with no controlling purpose or destination, creating traffic jams in my schedule.

One winter I was scheduled to speak at Houghton College in New York. Word reached me that weather had closed the Buffalo airport — they had 20 inches of snow on the ground. I took the initiative to reschedule a flight to Rochester.

That afternoon I left Greenville, South Carolina, and flew to Atlanta. After boarding another flight there, the stewardess informed the passengers that takeoff would be delayed due to mechanical problems.

I was worried that the Rochester airport might close at any time. I knew the New York thruway and other major highways were closed, and I was concerned about the 60-mile trip from Rochester to Houghton, knowing there would be whiteouts from high wind and drifting snow. I needed to arrive, to get the feel of the situation, to prepare for my first address the following morning.

The Boeing 737 was crowded. I was seated in the coach section, tucked in between two burly, strapping men whose dimensions required all their seat space and part of mine. Neither of them wished to talk.

The pilot kept announcing that the work crew was almost finished and takeoff would come shortly. At first I interpreted "shortly" to mean something like three minutes. But the minutes dragged into hours — three hours! I read the afternoon paper and two magazines from the rack. After that I had little else to do but sit still and be impatient.

Like a stubborn brat, I fretted and fumed. I must have waited more than two hours before switching over to the Christ-pleasing motive. When I finally did, I was hit with a reassuring realization that my bigger plans in life had not been grounded. I had something transcendent to live for. Though my body was still on the runway, my spirit could soar. My entire purpose for the trip in the first place was to serve Christ. Now I had an unexpected opportunity to serve Him in a different way. I could please Him by having a patient attitude. Even though my schedule was disrupted, I felt good about my life.

Professional pride

In an earlier chapter I distinguished between two kinds of pride—arrogance opposite humility and self-respect opposite shame. Both can be called pride.

Personal pride in one's appearance may be conceit for one person. For another person it might be respect for his or her associates at the office. In the one case it may stem from arrogance; in the other it may be from modesty. For the first individual it is a matter of vanity, but for the second it is a matter of personal dignity and honorable self-respect.

As the two kinds of pride relate to professional ego, the line between the two is often fuzzy. There is a worthy kind of pride a person should take in his or her work, a pride that is perfectly compatible with humility. The other kind of pride is self-serving; it rides on self-centeredness and egotism.

The desire for recognition, achievement and distinction is a legitimate human emotional desire, the same as the physical desire for food, sex or rest. It is not more wrong to enjoy a sense of fulfillment from passing an achievement test than it is to enjoy filet mignon, sex in marriage or a comfortable bed. No one should feel guilty for having the emotional desire for recognition or for feeling good when praised by a superior.

Temptation can appeal to this legitimate desire, however, resulting in the most defiling sort of arrogance. Strange as it may seem, the most unfulfilled underachiever often has the greatest problem with this temptation. The man who has made his mark in life, the woman who has succeeded as a professional—these are often the most humble people.

During a recent speaking engagement, I overheard the pastor say something complimentary about my preaching. It took no effort on my part to feel a pleasant sensation. The feeling was natural, not wrong. But then I began nourishing the emotion, drooling over the compliment, rolling it over in my mind like a gumdrop on the tongue. Legitimate self-respect began to shift to selfish pride. Temptation had caught me in a vulnerable position and attacked. All this took place in less than two minutes.

Quickly I made my move and switched over to the desire to please Christ. Though dormant for the last few minutes, the desire was still there, intact, preserved by the indwelling Spirit of God.

What followed was surprising. The unholy pride that was rising seemed almost instantly to fade out. I had pride one minute and humility the next. Now the exaggerated interest in the compliment seemed amusing. What I now had was not a superficial, trumped-up humility; it felt more like the real *me*. I felt at home with the feeling, comfortable with it. My yearning to please Christ made me wonder how I could have been so interested in myself. The trace of arrogance now seemed so unworthy, so thin and cheap, almost silly. Now I felt more important from

Christ's approval than from the pastor's—Christ's opinion meant more than his. The smile of Christ more than adequately fulfilled my human need for recognition.

Suppose, however, that instead of a compliment I had heard a criticism. I am sure I would have felt bad. My need for recognition would have been sadly unfulfilled. Yet the hurt feeling from the criticism would have been no more sinful than the good feeling from the compliment.

Few persons are mature enough to be immune from insults. If I had nourished and cultivated the hurt until it became resentment or hostility, it would have been sin. But if I had switched over to my deeper desire, the comfort of God's smile would have refortified my spirit. I know, for I have had criticism, too.

Jealousy

Carnal pride expresses itself not only in resentment and hostility, as mentioned above—it can also erupt in jealousy. Here I am not speaking of jealousy as vigilance in guarding something cherished, but as vindictive rivalry.

Almost every year for 25 years I have shared the platform with other speakers on various occasions. Many of my speaking engagements are at summer camps with three special services each day. Two or three guest speakers alternate on a rotating schedule for 10 days. Inevitably the listeners decide in their minds which preacher they think is best.

Some of these services are evangelistic in nature, with a strong emphasis on winning Christian converts. The preacher who has the most response to his public invitation to "come forward" is often considered by those in the pew as the most successful.

To ask the visiting speakers not to want to be successful would be asking too much. And there is nothing particularly unholy about wanting to be considered successful. While most of the preachers I have worked with do not wish to be competitive, the structure fosters competition. Congregational approval often comes at the other speakers' expense.

I do not think I ever wished to see my platform colleagues look bad. But I did not particularly mind having the congregation think I was pretty good. When I think of the sacredness and weightiness of the call to Christian ministry, anything competitive seems utterly cheap, yet I must confess to having felt this way sometimes. Much of my desire, however, was simply not to disappoint my hearers who, under God, had *given* me their time, their minds and, in a sense, their hearts for an hour. While feeling primarily responsible to God, I also felt accountable to the people who entrusted me with their time.

Whether I was ever jealous of a platform colleague, only God knows. Perhaps I have been. This much I know—year after year I was tormented with the temptation to feel competitive, needled with the urge to "make points" with the hearers, at times almost salivating to "score"—though I think I never compromised my message for audience approval.

What tormented me, however, was realizing that the temptation was there and feeling guilty over being tempted. The other pastors may have never been conditioned for such ego needs, and their temptation may have been minimal. But I needed to extricate myself from the entanglement.

One summer I was at a camp where a colleague had great audience appeal with his emotion-packed stories, the kind of appeal I considered cheap and refused to resort to. Here I finally came face-to-face with my problem and quit accusing myself for simply having a desire for approval.

I also concentrated my feelings on the desire to please Christ. I "homesteaded" on that desire. I let my full weight down, relaxing on it. I would go into a service acutely conscious of my *hope* to please Christ. I even got the feeling I would be thrilled with no response to my message and much response to my colleague's, if such response would please Christ.

I gave an invitation during one service, and I remember praying silently for no response if Christ could thereby be more glorified. When I gave a sermon that was obviously flat, I rejoiced in the occasion to prove my new attitude. When there was no response, I counted it pleasing to Christ if for no other reason than to teach me a lesson.

Though the surface temptation continued to appear from time to time, the problem was resolved. Switching over became easier and easier, and I rejoiced when the other preacher had great response. Now, before going into such a series, I set my house in order, reestablish my priorities and make every effort to keep one desire foremost in my thinking and feeling—the desire to please Christ.

In this chapter I have candidly exposed some of my temptations and vulnerabilities. Those who have never experienced these temptations can plug in their own. The sanctification motive to please Christ can become our "rock of refuge, to which [we] can always go" (Psalm 71:3).

11

Cultivating the Motive

DURING MY STUDENT PASTORING IN INDIANA, I visited an elderly gentleman on his small farm on the outer fringe of my parish. After I prayed with "Uncle Bud" and asked him to give his heart to Christ, he shared with me how at one time he had made a Christian commitment. For a period his life had been changed.

"The hardest job I ever did," he said, "was to cut bushes. And for a while I felt so good inside I even enjoyed cutting bushes." A faint smile traced his wrinkled face as he reflected on that experience.

Then he confessed, "I guess it's like raising corn. You've got to keep the ragweed out, and the jimson-weed and the crab grass. You've got to keep it culti-vated." Here he dropped his head for a long moment. Then he looked up, locking my eyes in his penetrat-ing gaze, and soberly announced, "I quit cultivating."

Established in the new motive

Sanctification is not the elimination of human de-sires, but it is eliminating their priority status. It is the elimination of the *area* of those desires that is *greater than* the desire to please Christ. To die as a martyr may require a much greater intensity of Christ-desire than merely to have a sanctified heart.

But to have a holy heart requires that the desire be stronger than everything else. Jesus did not say to Peter, "Do you love me?" He asked, "Do you love me more than these?" He did not say, "Seek the kingdom of God," but "Seek first the kingdom of God."

The excess, blown-up desire to satisfy human desires is what needs to be "crucified," "cleansed," "eliminated" or "replaced." In order for this to happen, those desires must either decrease or the Christ-desire must increase.

Sanctification, then, is the intensifying of the desire to please Christ to the point that it supersedes the desire to please self. This is the function of the Holy Spirit, but it also requires our cooperation. As this Christ-desire increases, the self-desires have a tendency to decrease. When the motive to please Christ crosses the line of being greater than the other desires, the Christian has experienced sanctification. Purification begins to flow through the person's spiritual system. Legitimate self-desires lose control, their position is usurped, their priority status is lost. Because he or she is attached to Christ, the Christian gains a measure of detachment from everything else.

While the new position is significant, no Christian has yet reached the point where he or she is immune to the possibility of returning to the old desires. When temptation appeals to these desires, they intensify. If the Christ-desire is only slightly greater than the self-desires, temptation becomes irresistible and a devastating civil war rages. The desire to please Christ, therefore, must be so much stronger than the others that it cannot be preempted by temptation. The secret of the victorious life is in *keeping* the motive to please Christ strong enough to withstand the temptation.

Once the position of sanctity is reached, it must be cultivated. There is absolutely no way to remain in a condition of sanctity without regular, rigorous practice of the motive to please Christ.

As a teenager on the farm I learned there were two purposes in cultivating the soil. One is to preserve moisture and fertilize the plants. The other is to weed out the competition—the "ragweed, jimsonweed and crab grass." One is positive and the other is negative.

In sanctification cultivation, the positive activity is to support the new desire to please Christ, "beefing it up," strengthening it, intensifying it, providing nutritional ingredients for its growth. The negative activity is to starve out competing desires, withholding their nutrition, minimizing their appeal, diluting their force.

Practical ethics

This cultivation is done two ways. The first way is by *practicing living from the deeper motive*, continually switching over. This establishes the pattern of the love-lifestyle.

After the newness of the desire was gone, I discovered my tendency to divorce it from practical ethics. Knowing Christ was pleased simply from my motive to please Him, I began resorting to the motive as a cover for not living it out. I even began feeling comfortable when my life was grossly displeasing to Him, somehow thinking He was still sufficiently pleased with my motive.

Then I began to see that the desire to please

Christ means striving to satisfy Him. Otherwise it is a phony desire. The motive has to be objectified to make sense. The desire to please Him has to be *a desire to please Him*, not simply a desire to have the desire. Without the effort to make it practical, the motive is vague, nebulous, indefinite and imprecise. Without being activated, the desire is too theoretical to become a driving, motivating force in a person's life. By putting it into practice, the motive thrives.

Living out the desire to please Christ and applying the motive to real-life situations fortifies the motive, establishing it as an operating base in a person's life.

Consolidating the feelings

The second way to cultivate the desire is *by devotional exercises*: feeding the mind with God's Word, becoming interested in God's interests, consolidating emotional feelings for Christ on the desire to please Him. God's Spirit is helping in every way. As a person comes to know Christ more intimately and to live with Him more closely, he or she comes more and more to think His thoughts and feel His feelings. The individual is in the process of settling down on the desire to please Him and consolidating feelings on that motive.

Here we must be careful to note the difference between our emotional feelings and our desire to please Christ. To be sure, much of the desire is from feeling, but it goes far beyond that. Included is a moral choice, a commitment, a surrender that is not exclusively the product of feeling.

In an earlier book, I made the point that real love is more morally than emotionally motivated—that it is more a matter of choice than of feeling.[13] While our desire to please Christ may not be totally separate from sentiment, it is grounded basically in moral choice. Feelings are often attached to the motive. They support the motive and make it more obvious, but they are not the basic ingredients of the motive.

Therefore we should not think the desire to please Christ is diminished when the emotional involvement has subsided. Emotions become thin and threadbare, at times overworked and incapable of strong feelings.

We are creatures of feeling, though, and our emotions are generally active. It is only sensible, therefore, to make special effort to attach our emotions to something worthwhile, to guard them and prevent them from becoming too involved with unworthy values. This is part of God's project in our lives.

We have often heard that the human race is incurably religious. Having been made in the divine image, we have religious ideals and feelings. These feelings need to be cultivated, not suppressed. But the danger is that they can be attached to unworthy ideals or to cultural, ethnic or generational traditions.

But who is more worthy of our feelings than the Lord Jesus Christ? What could be a nobler ideal to capture our feelings than the desire to please Christ? The object is to strengthen our motive to please Him. This highest of desires needs to be cultivated. It can be done most easily, most normally, with least personality conflicts by consolidating our feelings for Him.

Of course, other religious feelings need to be cultivated as well. At times we need to rest in His love for us, perhaps not conscious at all of our desire to please Him — only feeling the support and security of being loved by Him. A variety of religious feelings keeps our spiritual lives fresh and invigorating.

Getting to know Christ personally

When I was single a lovely female student whose name was Sheila came to my attention. I had only seen her one time from a distance, but others who knew her began to tell me about her. The more I learned, the more I decided I wanted to get to know her. But I had no idea if I wanted to share a lifetime with her — I did not know her yet.

One day we met. I discovered that her personality was even brighter than her smile and that her character was better than her good reputation. We became friends, and later I asked her to marry me.

After years of married life, I am still exploring her personality and still discovering happy surprises. The more we cultivate our relationship, the more brightness and goodness I discover. The better I know her the more I want to love her and the greater desire I have to please her.

As Christians most of us know what Christ is like. We have read the Bible and heard stories of how He has worked in people's lives. But only when we get to know Him in a spiritually intimate, personally satisfying way can we consolidate our feelings on Him, cultivating our motive to please Him.

When we do get to know Christ in this way, we first discover that His personality is bright, attractive and loving. But we also make an important discovery about ourselves. We learn that we can easily love Him.

Second, we realize that He is trustworthy and that

it is safe to commit our desires to Him. We need never feel apprehensive about surrendering our love to Him. While others may say they know *what* they believe, we can go further and say with Paul, "I know *whom* I have believed, and am convinced that he is able to keep what I have entrusted to him" (2 Timothy 1:12).

Christ is appealing and trustworthy, but we must cultivate our response to those qualities and keep ourselves sensitized to them. This is what I mean by devotional cultivation. Our feelings are consolidated on Him and on the desire to please Him by consistent fellowship. In this fellowship we are on the "frontier," exploring the divine personality!

Liberated!

FOR DAYS THE ACUTE SENSE of freedom remained. I had never dreamed I could feel so liberated from myself! It was one of the unexpected benefits from my experience in the college grove.

For so long I had been driven relentlessly by selfish motives. Though somewhat refined by cultural inhibitions, I had become so accustomed to accommodating myself that it seemed normal. I hardly had any idea there was another way to live. Like a drug addict desperate for the needle, I was on a crusade to placate my own desires, all the while only half aware of my crusade.

When I returned to my room, it was as if I had been let out of prison. Not having to accommodate myself felt good. I was free *not* to have to have the last word, to make the biggest point or to leave the greatest impression. I felt free not to express dissatisfaction with close friends or family members.

No longer did I have to defend myself. I felt free to be vulnerable! I was free from self-protectiveness. I did not have to grit my teeth and resist what offended my selfish ego. No longer was I my own slave. Having surrendered myself to Christ, I had nothing to protect. My new world felt so big, so open, so bright! It felt good to be defenseless!

Quite automatically I began detesting myself less and enjoying myself more. I did not have to go to the trouble to resist offense, and I liked myself for not putting me to the trouble. My self and I became better friends.

Now I could live, love, serve Christ, preach and help others without the self-serving motive lurking in the background. I had prestige with God without having to prop up my self-image.

Emotional hang-ups

For me, release from the inflated motive to please my human desires was dramatic. I have not overstated my case, though I have shared in earlier chapters how constant effort was required to live it out.

This new freedom, however, raises questions about how the new motive to please Christ deals with preconditioned emotional complications like bruised feelings, obsessions and personality patterns. No one should infer from what I have said above that these problems are automatically eliminated.

Rather than abolishing damaged emotions and entrenched patterns, the new motive shifts a person's focus to Christ. Personal priorities are changed. In this way a person is liberated from their stranglehold.

Until replaced by the motive to please Christ, these problems thrive on personal self-interests. Many of them developed in the first place at least partly from self-centered motives. Now the ground on which they stand is taken away. For a time many of them may remain, but they have lost their debilitating force. While not being freed from their presence, the surrendered Christian is freed from their power.

The new motive provides an inner climate in which, first, *damaged emotions* can ultimately be healed. Most bruised feelings result from inadequate fulfillment of basic emotional needs—failure to achieve, inadequate recognition, insufficient security, disappointment, rejection and deprivation of love.

With the shift of attention from self to Christ, the emotions discover a new support system—affirmation, security, acceptance and love. They are given new content for the healing process. Having lost their priority position, they do not tantalize and torment the committed Christian who focuses attention beyond him or herself to Christ.

Second, the new motive provides a system by which many *obsessions* can be both defused and diffused. No claim is here made that psychological compulsions automatically disappear when the new motive is acquired (though the new motive does provide a platform for therapy). But many obsessions have developed simply from excessive interest, attention and desire on one's self. These obsessions are diffused by shifting interest and desire to pleasing Christ. Emancipation from them comes from being "obsessed" with Christ.

Third, the intensified desire to please Christ enables a person to deal with old *personality patterns*. In chapter 2 I showed how these patterns often remain after the new motive is in place and functioning. Freedom does not come immediately. But with a shift of values and a new operating base, patterns are formed that replace the old patterns. It comes from "hanging in there" with the new motive "with all you've got," leaning on Christ for grit and grace to do it consistently.

The more firmly entrenched these old patterns have become, the longer it may take for them to be replaced. The person who early in life begins living from the love motive may never know what it means to be enslaved by such strong self-centered patterns. Those who allow nearly unbreakable habits to form are committing moral suicide.

In this chapter I am emphasizing how the Christ-love motive can liberate a person from psychological quirks and emotional entanglements. This is not to minimize, however, the direct assistance of God's Spirit and the availability of divine resources, without which we could never have shifted to the new motive in the first place, and without which our patterns can never be brought under the motive to please Christ.

Insecurities and despondency

Christian sanctification not only provides a base for achieving freedom from preconditioned emotional hang-ups, it also enables a person to break loose from situational emotional problems such as insecurity, dejection and failure.

Because we feel secure in our marriage, our home and family, our vocation or our community position, we start depending on these things for our security. We attach our feelings to them, desiring them for security's sake. We feel so secure in our human love relationships that our desire for Christ becomes vapid.

Fortunate are people whose false securities collapse in time to drive them to Christ. For many who get in the habit of preferring human securities, disappointment does not come soon enough. Their false props stand until old age or disease or death. By this time life has slipped into history, largely unlived.

Living from the Christ-love motive liberates us from our false securities. We shift our anchor. We stand above the world. Then it frees us from the *insecurities* of the world, from disappointment when our human securities fail. Deep down, where pretense is impossible, our insecurities give way to the security we have in Christ.

Similarly, despondency loses its sharpest sting when we are affixed to the desire to please Christ. The feeling is soothed.

Often when I feel dejected or disheartened, I attempt to "appropriate" Christ's presence. Simply feeling He is moving toward me helps dispel despondency. This is always proper and suitable, not carnally selfish.

While His presence always comforts my dejected spirit, it does not generally lift me out of dejection. It only "tides me over," giving me something to lean on without changing my emotional state. What do I mean?

Not long after my experience in the college grove, my feelings had "bottomed out" over something that I felt, at the time, was extremely important. Instead of seeking to appropriate His presence for pleasing *myself*, I decided to become interested in pleasing *Him*. My prayer was not "Come comfort me," but "Is there a way I can comfort You?" It was not "Come please me," but rather "How can I please You?"

Again, my emotions responded with an unexpected surprise. Rising out of myself, I was lifted from my gloom. I had something that captured my delight. That something was a Person, Jesus Christ. I had lost my self-consciousness in God-consciousness. My fixation on my problems was displaced by my preoccupation with His pleasure.

Human failures

Third, grounding our feelings on the desire to please Christ drastically reduces emotional vulnerability to human failure. We all have friends who believe in us, whose confidence deserves to be honored. We do not wish to let them down. When I know I have disappointed them, I feel greatly disappointed with myself.

As I mentioned earlier, I have many opportunities to speak in churches and at camps and colleges. Local people have anticipated, planned and prepared for the event, and then they have sacrificed to attend. I want them to be pleased with what I have to say (what the Holy Spirit has to say through me)— not for my sake but for theirs. I want them to get something out of my ministry and not be disappointed. But they are only pleased with a good message, not my good intentions.

When I feel I am disappointing people I would like to please, I have a tendency to blame them for expecting too much. I start feeling victimized by their excessive anticipations. But when I look at the situation objectively, I often realize that their expectations are not too high—I am simply unable to deliver. Then I feel put down by my own inadequacies, sometimes mercilessly accusing myself.

By this time my only recourse is to switch over— from my desire to please them to my desire to please

God. He is pleased with my good motive even when He is not satisfied with my performance. I am not "utterly cast down" (Psalm 37:24, KJV). I can admit to myself my own inadequacy without being devastated by the admission. I am still pleasing Christ, and this is my first desire. On my highest priority I have not failed.

Living on our desire to please Christ reduces our need for emotional props; it contributes to our basic emotional needs. We have a source for regular emotional lift—the smile of God. Knowing He is pleased gratifies our greatest desire. We have "set [our] minds on things above, not on earthly things" (Colossians 3:2).

And What about My Neighbor?

IN MY NEW INTRIGUE WITH CHRIST, I soon discovered that my interest in pleasing other people diminished. I was relieved to feel less peer pressure. I could resort to the smile of Jesus without requiring the approval of others. Being responsible only to Christ simplified my agenda.

The problem was that being snug and cozy felt too good. I began to feel detached from the needs of the world. I became aloof, indifferent toward human relationships, complacent toward those who hurt. *Snug*ness became *smug*ness.

In an earlier chapter I stated that human sociality is a reflection of divine sociality, which was eternally fulfilled in the Trinity. The notion of creation, however, shows that God's social nature extends beyond the Trinity. He created us for fellowship, for a love relationship with Himself and for participation in His eternal glory.

If God's social nature extends beyond the Trinity, surely our social nature (which derives from His) is not limited to fellowship with Him. John wrote, "For anyone who does not love his brother, whom he has seen, cannot love God, whom he has not seen. And he has given us this commandment: Whoever loves God must also love his brother" (1 John 4:20–21). Paul said, "Each of us should please his neighbor" (Romans 15:2).

For years many of my relationships had been built on self-serving motives. I had reached out only to those whose love I considered worthwhile. But I had few resources for relating with unlovable and unattractive personalities. The kind of love I had for others could not absorb rebuff and rebuke. It left me vulnerable to bitterness. I was programmed for hostility when my self-centered love was rejected or betrayed.

The acid test of Christian love is in the nitty-gritty struggle of human relationships. "If it weren't for my neighbors," said one woman, "I would love everybody."

My smug aloofness to the opinions of others was soon checked by my new love for Christ. The Holy Spirit had deposited in my being a love that saturated my sympathies and began to permeate my relationships. Self-serving love seemed deactivated. I became more other-conscious and less self-centered. It was easier to accept people for who they were, setting no conditions, requiring no agenda, demanding no response. God's love in my heart dissolved a large measure of my touchiness and sensitivity. Pleasing my neighbor became interesting activity.

Again, I am not claiming instant restructuring of entrenched personality patterns. What I am claiming is a foundation for functioning relationships. It is nothing I deserve credit for. I was hooked on hostility. Alone I was unable to kick the habit. God has done something in me that I could not do for myself.

The love of Christ has freed me from those hate hooks. I am no longer a hostage to hostility. Paul announced, "God has poured out his love into our hearts by the Holy Spirit, whom he has given us" (Romans 5:5).

From this fertility, friendships thrive. John wrote, "If we love one another, God lives in us and his love is made complete in us. We know that we live in him and he in us, because he has given us his Spirit" (1 John 4:12-13).

Helping the hurting

The new love motive, however, had social dimensions beyond functional relationships. As I attempted to practice my love for Christ, I discovered a new tenderness toward the feelings of others. Freed from exorbitant self-concern, I developed the ability to hurt with those who hurt. Soon I discovered that aloofness toward human need is incongruent with love for Christ.

The social implications of pleasing Christ are too obvious to miss. Jesus spoke of feeding the hungry, giving water to the thirsty, befriending the friendless, clothing those who are naked, ministering to the ill, visiting prisoners. Then He made a startling proclamation: "I tell you the truth, whatever you did for one of the least of these brothers of mine, you did for me. . . . whatever you did not do for one of the least of these, you did not do for me" (Matthew 25:34-46).

The Christian who has made pleasing Christ a priority cannot escape the compulsion. Jesus Christ so identified with the poor, the diseased and the hungry that we who love Him must love as He loves. The second great commandment—"Love your neighbor as yourself"—immediately follows the first—"Love the Lord your God with all your heart" (Matthew 22:37–39). Jesus specifically said, "The second is like [the first]." The two are inseparable.

The vertical and horizontal go together. One beam of Christ's cross reaches toward God; the arms of the other point to the world. At the cross the two directions were riveted together. Loving God has a social dimension. Loving others has a divine mandate.

What motivated the Belgian priest to give his life for the lepers on the island of Molokai, knowing he himself would die a victim of leprosy? Where does Mother Teresa draw resources to carry in her heart Calcutta's diseased and dying with no plans of a comfortable retirement? How do we explain the work of thousands of missionaries who expend their lives ministering to people in isolated, remote places without mid-life burnout?

The command to love our fellow humans, standing alone, is inadequate. Obeying the command requires hearts aflame with love that only Christ can give. Responding to His love, we also respond to the people He loves.

Tonight millions of people will go to bed hungry, many of them approaching death from malnutrition. Most are committed to no political agenda. Denied the "indulgence" of convenience, adequate nutrition and barest necessities, they struggle on against impossible odds, consumed with the hope for survival. These our neighbors on this tiny planet hopelessly cling to hope. The haunting words of Jeremiah prick our complacency: "Is it nothing to you, all you who pass by?" (Lamentations 1:12).

At our fingertips each day are many who silently bleed, waiting for love and sacrifice. To believe we can really love Christ and remain indifferent toward the needs of others is difficult. By serving them we serve Christ, and our desire to please Him finds a way to express itself.

This is precisely the problem with many Christians — they enjoy God's love but have barely reciprocated. They enjoy personal salvation but have stopped short of sanctification. They have been pleased by Christ but have little desire to please Him. Self-centered rather than Christ-centered, they have no motive to help those whom Christ loves.

Christian evangelism

What I have called the social implications of sanctification include much more than physical, economic and medical concerns. Caring for people involves concern for their emotional and spiritual needs.

Multiplied millions have no personal knowledge of Jesus Christ. Saddled with guilt, tormented with meaninglessness, plagued with existential fears, they have no peace, little hope and no assurance of eternal life. Does it make sense for us to improve their living conditions without sharing the Christ who can change their lives on a deeper level? Being human includes a transcendent spirit as much as a physical body. Consequently we cannot be genuinely humanitarian and neglect spiritual needs any more than we can be Christian and neglect the physical and social.

Some of us consider the spiritual to be more basic, but physical needs are often more acutely felt. Helping people in this area, therefore, can become a tool for evangelism. When they respond to economic help, they often bring their whole persons, spiritual as well as physical. Being a friend positions you to lead the one you have befriended to the feet of Christ.

After I had been married a few months, it hit me with great force that I had married much more than my bride. I had to live with her interests and her likes and dislikes. Her friends became my friends, her family my family.

At first, loving Christ seemed so simple. Then we discover more than we expected. Loving Christ includes more than loving Christ; those He loves are also included in the arrangement. When our lives are programmed with the love of God, loving our neighbor is a part of the program.

14

Ultimate Fulfillment

For days I had worked on my junior high science project, expecting to win first prize. I had spent more time, I figured, than most of the other students. The fun had come from the expectation of reward, not from creative accomplishment. One girl even remarked disdainfully, "He's so sure he's going to win."

When the award day came, the bottom fell out of my world. I did not win the prize.

My friends were still happy, even though they had not won either. I had worked hard, and now I felt terrible. They had done little and were feeling great—probably because they did not expect to win.

Disappointment

Unfulfilled expectations create inexpressible anguish. The harrowing distress is often too heavy to bear. At Superbowl time only two teams can compete for the final prize. Both teams have played and won many games to get to this point, but only one will go away the winner. The other team will leave disappointed, its hopes crushed in defeat.

Ask the losing team, though, and to a man, they will say that they would not have traded the experience for anything. They were willing to risk disappointment and defeat for the chance of victory. Without such risk life loses its adventure and challenge.

I cannot help feeling, however, that countless people fling themselves recklessly on unworthy goals simply because they have nothing better to reach for. Their search for fulfillment is like drinking salt water to slake thirst. They set themselves up for disappointment as if they were mice following a Pied Piper to destruction.

John Stuart Mill, English philosopher and economist, wrote:

> Those only are happy who have their minds fixed on some object other than their own happiness . . . followed not as a means but as itself an ideal end. Aiming thus at something else, they find happiness. . . . Ask yourself whether you are happy, and you cease to be so. The only chance is to treat, not happiness, but some end external to it, as the purpose of life.[14]

The problem is with the "external end" that we choose. If our highest priority is a bank account, good health, creative activity, family or friends, we set ourselves up for disappointment and unhappiness. As a controlling purpose in life, these values are completely inadequate.

What we need is a purpose not only transcendent enough to satisfy our spirits, but also solid enough to command our confidence.

A higher hope

The singers of Israel repeated a refrain: "Why are you downcast, O my soul? Why so disturbed within me? *Put your hope in God,* for I will yet praise him, my Savior and my God" (Psalm 42:5,11; 43:5; italics added).

Placing our hope in any other person or thing is dangerous. But when our highest hopes are placed in God, there will be no disappointment, no reason to be "cast down." His countenance is uplifting. His smile dispels gloom, penetrates darkness and bathes the human soul with a light than cannot be dimmed. And when we hope in God, there is less dissatisfaction from other unfulfilled hopes.

When my highest purpose is to please Christ, my greatest expectation is to see His smile; my fondest hope is to contribute to His pleasure. Then I need not be disappointed. I can absorb the lower disappointments because they resulted only from lesser desires. I can still be happy when I have lost the ball game, not because of the loss but in spite of it— because I have a greater desire from which I function. My highest delight is the divine smile.

If this motive is the operating base for our lives, all lesser hopes, desires and purposes have to take second place. Surely divine approval can absorb all lesser disappointments. It is like saving one's life precisely by losing it. By surrendering popcorn, peanuts and potato chips, we gain a banquet of exquisite cuisine!

At age 22, while engaged in three months of mission work on the Isle of Pines (an island west of Cuba in the Caribbean), I wrote in my journal: "How pleased I would be if God should call me to work on the mission field through life! I'd love to labor, unrewarded, among these people on foreign soil to help drive away their darkness."

Now as I read it over, I smell the flavor of youthful idealism, especially in that line about "loving to labor unrewarded." Since then, however, I have visited missionaries on various fields who are expending their lives to bring light to those in darkness. From them all, the same testimony keeps coming through: No labor for Christ is unrewarded! Pleasing Him is a pleasing experience. The reward is in His smile. That is worth everything!

At peace with the universe

When I look back across my life and recall certain unfulfilled hopes, unrealized dreams and disappointed expectations, they seem so small alongside those of people who have suffered so much more loss than I have suffered. But even what little I have known of suffering makes life seem incongruous and contradictory. Where is life's cohesive ingredient? Who is supposed to be lacing together the loose ends? Why is life's recurring refrain a continuing chant of broken dreams and buried hopes? And why is the refrain so disharmonious with the human spirit?

Yet I have noticed that these disappointments never come from the human spirit's highest goal—pleasing Jesus Christ. They occur from the lower purposes, goals and desires, many of which are worthy, but inferior to what should be our highest controlling goal.

When we place our hopes and wishes primarily in human relationships or earthly achievements, then in a sense our lives become "one" with those lower purposes. There we identify. When the hopes are broken our lives collapse.

But life was intended to be lived above this level. The human spirit is equipped to identify beyond the lower goals that can let us down. We are built to be "one" with ultimate reality, at peace with the Creator God who allows no contradictions.

Realizing the need for ultimate identity, Eastern mysticism has opted for a pantheism in which the person and his or her environment—the knower and the known—lose their separate identities and supposedly merge into one. But the peace the Eastern mystic realizes (if indeed peace is realized) comes primarily from simply overlooking the contradictions.

Christ has made available for us the possibility of identifying with His goals and purposes. Cooperating with everything that is ultimately inevitable, we ride with the flow. We are in harmony with living. We are "one" with universal reality. We have peace with a universe whose surface contradictions are dissolved in hopes that are not disappointed and in dreams that are consistently realized.

I used to sing to myself over and over again, "I'd rather have Jesus than anything this world affords today." The song still means much to me; I will never become aloof to that desire. But now I have added a stanza: "I'd rather *please* Jesus!" This desire is one up on the original. It is a higher category. Living above ourselves and focusing our desires beyond ourselves is the substance of Christian sanctity.

When we take God's purpose behind our lives and make it our greatest purpose in life, we begin to live as we were created to live. We fulfill the purpose for which we were made. Here we are at home with ourselves and with our universe. This at-homeness is not a resort. For us it becomes a permanent residence.

15

Final Success

THE STORIES ABOUT GEORGE WASHINGTON fascinated me as a child. Fathering an infant nation was surely the ultimate in success. My heroes were not Superman, Batman or Wonder Woman—my heroes were my dad and George Washington. To my childhood mind, nothing could exceed having your name on the lips of future generations. If only I could leave in my wake a fame that would follow me, my life would not have been in vain.

A controlling purpose

As a stabilizing force in life, everyone needs a single controlling purpose. Though we legitimately have many purposes in life, we need one overshadowing purpose to keep all other ambitions and desires in alignment. English novelist George Eliot has her character Philip Wakem say, "I think of too many things—sow all sorts of seeds, and get no great harvest from any one of them. . . . I flutter all ways, and fly in none."[15]

In today's world *success* is preeminent. "Making it big" has higher market value and carries more prestige than anything else. Success is measured by how much money a person makes and how far he or she has climbed the corporate ladder. Show business and sports personalities often predicate success on stardom. Whatever the criterion, no one wants to be a failure.

The problem with this mentality is that our attention is so focused on the visible order that we are blinded to the larger economy about us. We are nearsighted. We commit ourselves to perishing values. Our lives are sacrificed for wealth or fame, while on the higher level we are bankrupt and unknown.

Desperately trying to be *somebodies* in the world, we become *nobodies* in God's kingdom. We succeed in our inferior purposes but fail where it counts. Our lives are wasted.

Success with God

Sanctification means making glorifying God your controlling purpose. It means that pleasing Christ from the love motive is your highest priority.

Success, accomplishment and recognition are not necessarily evil desires. They are legitimate human ego-needs that can depend upon Christ's purposes for fulfillment. In another book I made the point that such ego-needs originate in the way we have been created for divine love and recognition.[16]

Success with God is infinitely more satisfying than success in the world. By identifying with God's purposes, the ego-needs are not fulfilled with egotism. They are fulfilled by seeing His goals succeed, His movement prosper, His kingdom come. You succeed by helping Him succeed. Your success is derived from His.

This can be compared, using the football analogy again, to a fan who attaches his ego to his favorite team. The team becomes his alter ego, and his ego-needs are fulfilled by the team's success. Sanctified Christians attach their egos to Christ, to His cause, to His success. Rather than being selfish or egotistic, they are liberated from egotism. Selfishness is dissolved by attaching the ego-needs to a selfless purpose that satisfies the needs.

You do not have to exalt yourself to be somebody special. You have placed your reputation in His hands and have identified your success with His. You have abandoned "being somebody" for yourself. You want to make Christ known as Somebody. You have "died" to the blown-up desire for a name; it has dissolved in your desire to make His name known and revered.

Countdown to success

Any purpose in life that is inferior to God's purpose, any success that is less than success with God, any accomplishment that does not contribute to God's pleasure and glory, is inadequate for ultimate fulfillment and does not contribute to a person's final success. Without this highest controlling motive, life is ultimately lived in vain.

In the long and frantic pursuit of economic, academic or professional accomplishment, there lingers for most people the nagging desire for their lives not to be ultimately wasted. Poetess Emily Dickinson wrote:

> If I can stop one Heart from breaking
> I shall not live in vain
> If I can ease one Life the Aching
> Or cool one Pain

Or help one fainting Robin
Unto his Nest again
I shall not live in Vain.[17]

In 1897 at the age of 25, my great uncle Quincy C. Murphree lay dying with typhoid fever and was told by his pastor, "Brother Quincy, do you know that you will be in heaven in a short time?"

He opened his eyes in apparent surprise, answering, "No." In less than an hour, he said, "Jesus is with me. I love Him. I adore Him. He is my Savior. Oh, that I could live to serve Him." Living to serve Christ was his dying wish. Soon he was gone.

Some of us have been afflicted with the desire to do something big for God. We have wanted to move mountains, to do something spectacular. Simply pleasing Christ has seemed too small to our sensational, success-oriented minds.

Yet the humble, unlearned servant of Christ may be in his or her own way fulfilling God's purpose and contributing to His pleasure as much as the person who wins wide acclaim for a successful ministry. At a news conference, Billy Graham once said, "If an inner-city mission worker is more faithful to his calling than I am to mine, his crown will shine more brightly in heaven than mine will shine."

John Milton, physically blind, wrote:

Doth God exact day-labor, light denied,
I fondly ask; but Patience, to prevent
That murmur, soon replies, God doth not need
Either man's work or his own gifts. Who best
Bears His mild yoke, they serve Him best. His
   state
Is kingly: thousands at His bidding speed,

And post o'er land and ocean without rest;
They also serve who only stand and wait.[18]

For many years I carried a heavy preaching load. Now God has led me to shift gears. Toccoa Falls College specializes in preparing students for Christian ministry. For me, teaching here is a distinctive ministry in itself. I still do much preaching and am involved in many other projects. My schedule is full, all with Christian ministry.

Yet in my early-morning devotions one day, I felt an almost overwhelming sense of uselessness. Perhaps it was withdrawal pains from my heavy pulpit schedule. Long ago I had lost the desire to be a "star," but having been called to ministry I did not want to feel that my usefulness had been curtailed. Of course, I had felt useless many times before, even while filling the pulpit on a daily schedule. But this time the feeling was acute. And it was frustrating.

As soon as I "switched over," the pain was mitigated. Though I had wanted to be a preacher since a young age, I realized that my highest calling was not to preach but to please Christ. That was my first purpose. I knew I was serving where God had chosen to position me, and I felt useful. My calling had not been disparaged. My life was still on course.

When your highest priority is to please Christ, you do not have to do what Christian society considers great things for God. You can make your contribution, large or small, and it becomes a part of the larger whole. Your effort, though unnoticed, is not wasted. Though unsung, you are still serving. In the overall economy of God's kingdom, your position is just as strategic as that of any other person. Your life is being invested in a cause that is infinitely worth-while. By contributing to the pleasure and glory of God, you are a success.

Only a foretaste

If I should gain great popularity and immense wealth, the respect of my acquaintances and acclaim from the world, if I should alleviate world hunger, reduce international tensions and turn multitudes to the Savior, all from an inferior motive, and end up not having contributed to the pleasure of Christ and the glory of God, my life will have been a monumental failure!

To me, Jesus Christ has become a real person. He is closer than the air I breathe. Everything I sense in His presence is immaculately beautiful, frighteningly adorable, creating in me a holy desire for highest worship. Yet what I now sense in Him is only a foretaste of what I am to know. Someday I will stand in His presence and see Him face-to-face. That awesome presence will then be rich, brighter than a thousand suns! If in that moment I can but catch a glimpse of a slight smile, my life will have been a mammoth success!

If in this life God can lead me through all my hang-ups, my personality entanglements, the emotional bondage that has enchained me, through my selfishness and sins, my hopelessness and despair, to that moment when I face Him—if at that moment He will turn toward me with a smile of approval, if I can sense that He is pleased with me, that I have contributed to His pleasure, I will then be satisfied a million times over!

The impossible will have taken place. My highest

desire will have been fulfilled. The Spirit-installed motive will have paid incalculable dividends. Returns on the investment will be eternal. The pleasure of having pleased Christ will stretch beyond imagination. The most improbable person in the world will have made it!

The pleasure of pleasing Christ, discovered in a college grove, will continue without end in worlds to come!

1. Richard Lovelace, "To Althea from Prison," in John L. Stoddard, ed., *The Stoddard Library*, Vol. 8 (Chicago and Boston: George L. Shuman & Co., 1910), p. 252.
2. F. Brook, "My Goal Is God Himself," *Hymns of the Christian Life* (Camp Hill, PA: Christian Publications, Inc., 1978), p. 265.
3. Aristotle, *Nicomachean Ethics*, Book IX, Chapter 8 in Richard McKeon, ed., *Introduction to Aristotle* (New York: Random House, 1947), pp. 508–511.
4. John R.W. Stott, "Am I Supposed to Love Myself or Hate Myself?" *Christianity Today* (April 20, 1984).
5. David K. Clark, "Philosophical Reflections on Self-Worth and Self-Love," *Journal of Psychology and Theology* (Spring, 1985), pp. 3–11.
6. C.S. Lewis, *God in the Dock* (Grand Rapids, MI: Wm. B. Eerdmans Publishing Co., 1970), p. 194.
7. Dennis F. Kinlaw, *Preaching in the Spirit* (Grand Rapids, MI: Francis Asbury Press of Zondervan, 1985), pp. 105–106, 108–109.
8. Quoted by C.S. Lewis, *Mere Christianity* (New York: MacMillian Publishing Co., 1960), p. 158.
9. Robert Browning, "Andrea del Sarto," *The Poems of Robert Browning* (London: Oxford University Press, 1928), p. 132.
10. C.S. Lewis, *Mere Christianity*, p. 160.
11. John Wesley, *A Plain Account of Christian Perfection* (London: The Epworth Press, 1952), pp. 33, 45, 109.
12. Wesley, p. 33.

13. Jon Tal Murphree, *Made to Be Mastered* (Grand Rapids, MI: Baker Book House, 1984), pp. 99–100.
14. John Stuart Mill, *Autobiography* (New York: Columbia University Press, 1924).
15. George Eliot, *The Mill on the Floss* (New York: Dodd, Mead & Co., 1960), pp. 319–320.
16. Jon Tal Murphree, *When God Says You're OK* (Downer's Grove, IL: Intervarsity Press, 1975), pp. 98–101.
17. Emily Dickinson, "If I can stop one Heart from breaking," *The Complete Poems of Emily Dickinson* (Boston and Toronto: Little, Brown and Company, 1960), p. 433.
18. John Milton, "On His Blindness," *The Complete Poems of John Milton* (New York: Bonanza Books, division of Crown Publishers, Inc., 1936), pp. 613–614.